HANDBOOK FOR LAY & SELF-SUPPORTING WORKERS

Heralding the Second Coming

Colin D Standish & Russell R Standish

Copyright © 2005 by Colin and Russell Standish
All rights reserved
Printed in United States of America

Hartland Publications
Box 1
Rapidan, Virginia, USA 22733

ISBN 0-923309-93-4

Handbook for
Lay and Self-Supporting Workers

1	The Focus of Non-Denominational Ministries	5
2	What Is Self-Supporting Lay Ministry?	7
3	The Call to Lay and Self-Supporting Work	14
4	A Brief History of Self-Supporting Work	23
5	Sensing a Need	29
6	Single Focused Self-Supporting Work	36
7	Individual and Family Self-Supporting Work	48
8	Larger Institutional Self-Supporting Ministries	55
9	Developing a College or an Academy	63
10	Establishing a Health Center	68
11	Establishing a Publishing and/or Printing House	79
12	Establishing a Media Ministry	85
13	Agriculture, the ABC of Ministry	93
14	Choosing Property	103
15	Developing the Physical Plant	112
16	Financing a New Project	120
17	Developing Financial Support	125
18	Seminars, Camps and Convocations	133
19	The Organizational Chart	138
20	Governance in Self-Supporting Work	149
21	The Choice of Staff	157
22	The Applicant Interview	163
23	In-Service Training of Institutional Personnel	170
24	Accreditations and Affiliations	174
25	Moral Rectitude	179
26	Living and Working Together	186
27	Principles for Addressing the Erring	193
28	Dealing with Suspected Misconduct	198
29	Applying Biblical Principles	210
30	Why God-Raised-Up Institutions Fail	216

Chapter 1

The Focus of Non-Denominational Ministries

FIRST and foremost, the underlying principle of this handbook is the unwavering concept of the authors in the Protestant belief in the priesthood of all believers. The unity of goals and service between ministry and laity is clearly expressed in the equality of all God's children before our Master.

> But be not ye called Rabbi: for one is your Master, even Christ; and all ye are brethren.   Matthew 23:8

If we are all brethren, then we are one in ministry and one in all soul-saving endeavors. The watch-cry of the Reformation was the "priesthood of all believers." Such a Protestant declaration reverberated in the words of the early pioneers of the Seventh-day Adventist Church. Thus they declared, "We have no pope or potentate; we have no creed other than the Bible." However, such declarations placed solemn responsibilities upon the laity. Inherent in these dictums are:

1   Personal decision making as central to the acceptance of Christ's salvation.
2   Daily and prayerful study of God's Word to search out the vital beliefs and practices enshrined in Holy Scripture.
3   To live out these truths in the power of the indwelling Christ.
4   The responsibility to share these precious truths actively with others.

This handbook is about mission and ministry. It is not a stereotype or binding manual but rather simple guidelines and suggestions which we have learned by test and trial over many years of leadership in denominational and lay ministries and by observing many other leaders, both successful and unsuccessful.

Hopefully we have learned well the counsels and application of Divine instruction; and where inspiration is silent, we have sought to learn from the successful practices which have been achieved in our own ministries as well as the ministries of others. Further, we have sought to learn from our mistakes and the mistakes of others.

We have designed this handbook to be very practical, with summaries following each chapter. The theory and divine counsel is shared when applicable, and the handbook is liberally sprinkled with references to stories of various ministers to add focus and practical suggestions.

We sincerely pray that this handbook will inspire you to find the vision of God's calling for you. We further pray that it will be a great blessing in helping you to avoid the pitfalls which others have experienced, and generate ideas that will lead to a successful ministry. For those who are already engaged in self-supporting and lay ministries, our goal is to offer ideas or suggestions which will form the foundation of the strengthening of your ministry. This is a handbook both for those who have not yet begun a ministry and those who desire to enhance the effectiveness of the ministry which they have already established. We have to keep in focus so that no matter what ministry you have chosen, the ultimate goal is to lead men and women to the kingdom of Christ.

God bless you, and may the Holy Spirit guide you, and may many souls be rescued from the clutches of Satan as a result of your ministry.

Chapter 2

What Is Self-Supporting Lay Ministry?

SOME years ago, Colin was travelling with a prominent self-supporting leader from France. As they traveled, he expressed an interest in Colin's concept of self-supporting work. He said his understanding had been forged in dialogue with a leader from the Euro-Africa Division. It would seem that this leader had explained that the Division would be supportive of his work and ministry providing that it did not duplicate the work of the denomination.

Upon inquiry, Colin discovered what had been specifically excluded had been the publishing work, public evangelistic work, and the educational training work. Colin marveled that this self-supporting leader believed these to be valid exclusions. Yet he presented no inspired evidence to support this understanding and, indeed, we have never discovered such restrictions.

The scope of self-supporting work is not different from denominational work. It encompasses the same soul-saving ministries. In reality, that which this division leader had permitted the self-supporting leader to pursue was confined to restaurant work and health ministry. We assume that this division leader had little interest in restaurant and health ministry. However, these ministries should be just as much a part of denominational enterprises as they are of self-supporting enterprises. The two are not in conflict, rather each is supplemental to the other. Self-supporting work is just as strongly mandated by God as is denominational work. God sees the need for both. Indeed, as the time approaches for the final thrust or the worldwide spread of the three angels' messages, it will be humble servants led by the Holy Spirit who will dominate the ranks of God's messengers.

> Thus the message of the third angel will be proclaimed. As the time comes for it to be given with greatest power, the Lord will work through humble instruments, leading the minds of those who consecrate themselves to His service. The laborers will be qualified rather by the unction of His Spirit than by the training of literary institutions. Men of faith and prayer will be constrained to go forth with holy zeal, declaring the words which God gives them. The sins of Babylon will be laid open.
> *Great Controversy*, 606

God has ordained that both denominational and self-supporting workers shall labor for the common goal to spread the everlasting gospel to the world. It is not that one works under the other, but that both work together under the same gospel commission of Christ and the promptings of the Holy Spirit. Properly following the designs of God, the denominational workers and the self-supporting laborers will minister hand in hand, each honoring the call of the other and the contributions which each is making to the finishing of God's work. There must be no rivalry between the two. Rather, there must be close cooperation. There is no ministry which is the purview of the denominational work and another kind of ministry which is the purview of the self-supporting work. All the major arms of the work—evangelism, educational, publishing, colporteuring, health and temperance—are to engage the attention and active service of all God's people.

Denominational ministry, properly pursued, possesses some decided advantages. First, the members serving in this capacity have been chosen by a wider body of believers. Denominational workers have been directly chosen to be the servant leaders of the work of God. They have a second advantage; they have access to much greater resources than most self-supporting ministries have available to them and therefore, generally speaking, are able to attempt the larger projects and major outreaches to the world. They have as their backing the tithes and offerings of the great majority of active church members.

On the other hand, self-supporting work, by its very nature, has advantages that are rarely available to denominational workers. Because these ministries are generally small and are rarely encumbered by complicated organizational machinery, lay workers are able to respond quickly and effectively to the needs and the calls which they receive. Self-supporting workers, further, generally speaking, have a much greater freedom to decide where they will serve and in what capacity they will labor. Unencumbered by the pressure to remain silent in times of spiritual crisis, as is so often witnessed among denominational employees, self-supporting workers are much more likely and are in a far better position to heed God's command to "Cry aloud, spare not, lift up thy voice like a trumpet" (Isaiah 58:1). Further, self-supporting workers, because of the self-sacrificing service of most of those involved in this work, are able to accomplish much more for a significantly reduced outlay of funds than denominational work. Their self-supporting work is, in general, much more cost effective.

However, there are also dangers, often grave dangers, in both denominational and self-supporting work. These dangers were all too obvious to Colin in the sixteen years he served in denominational work and the twenty-six years he has served in self-supporting work. Russell experienced the same in thirty-one years of denominational employment and eleven in self-supporting service. The dangers in denominational work include an hierarchical mentality in which leaders believe that they have the right to micro-manage and control the field laborers in the details of their ministry, methods, and their field of service. Sister White warns of these dangers which had become reality in her day.

> God has not set any kingly power in the Seventh-day Adventist Church to control the whole body, or to control any branch of the work. He has not provided that the burden of leadership shall rest upon a few men. Responsibilities are distributed among a large

number of competent men.
Christian Leadership, 49

In the work of the Lord for these last days there should be no Jerusalem centers, no kingly power. And the work in the different countries is not to be bound by contracts to the work centering in Battle Creek, for this is not God's plan. Brethren are to counsel together, for we are just as much under the control of God in one part of His vineyard as in another. *The Publishing Ministry*, 130

Too much power is invested in humanity when matters are so arranged that one man or a small group of men have it in their power to rule or ruin the work of their fellow laborers. . . . The kingly power formerly exhibited in the General Conference is not to be perpetuated.
Spalding and Magan Collection, 368

James White, before he died in 1881, gave a salutary warning that this was not to be the case. Here is his startling statement.

The minister who throws himself on any conference committee for direction, takes himself out of the hands of Christ. *Review and Herald*, January 4, 1881

There is great danger in denominational work that men will believe that administrative and conference office responsibilities are prizes for which to strive as they climb the ladder of upward mobility. Often these posts are judged to be of more importance than the work in the field—Bible work, soul-winning work, colporteur ministry, and public evangelism.

This leads to the third great danger in denominational work—the politicizing of the work, especially for those whose ambitions are not so much for "the Master's glory" (Messages to Young People, 100) but are for the selfish goals of the individual which leads to tragic consequences where the work of

God is greatly diminished and greatly perverted.

It is very difficult, and takes extraordinary courage today, for denominational employees to stand up and speak out against apostasy, wickedness, and worldliness in God's church, for so often this is falsely seen as disloyalty to "the church."

Yet another danger in denominational work has resulted from the fearful success of the introduction of the liberal agenda of apostasy, lowered Christian standards, and blasphemous worship patterns into God's church.

On the other hand, there are serious dangers in self-supporting work. Self-supporting work can generate an independence which is ungodly, an independence which separates the workers from counseling closely with others. This independence often takes the form of the denunciation of denominational work and, for that matter, others who are working in self-supporting work. It also can lead to competition for the financial support of the laity and engender the belief that one's own ministry is more important than any other ministry. Self-supporting work, through this independence, has often been a fertile field for the sowing and germinating of deadly winds of doctrine which are fatal to Christian growth and Christian unity. Not uncommonly, self-supporting leaders also exercise kingly power no less ruthlessly than some denominational leaders exercise such power.

The summary of these observations is that both denominational and self-supporting work is readily perverted when in the hands of undedicated and ambitious, worldly-motivated men and women. We do not need to make a mistake by declaring that one or other is the only right way to accomplish the calling which God has placed upon men and women. Neither those in denominational nor self-supporting work can declare that one or the other is the only way to accomplish the completion of the task. This is the time for faithful, earnest, sincere and committed Seventh-day Adventists in both denominational and lay ministry to link hands together for the hastening of the coming of Jesus and the completion of the gospel commission.

SUMMARY

1. All Christians are called to the ministry of Jesus Christ.
2. There is no qualitative difference between the ministry to which laity and pastors are called.
3. Advantages of denominational ministry include:
   a. They have been chosen by a wider body of believers.
   b. Frequently they have greater resources at their disposal
   c. They are in a better position to attempt to undertake larger projects.
   d. They have the financial resource of most active members' tithes and offerings.
4. Advantages of lay ministries:
   a. They are rarely encumbered by complicated organizational machinery.
   b. They are able to respond more quickly to calls for urgent needs.
   c. They have greater freedom to follow the Holy Spirit's leading in their calling.
   d. They are in a better position to give God's people the warning message.
   e. Their ministry is accomplished at significantly less cost because of sacrifice.
5. Dangers commonly found in denominational work:
   a. The exercising of kingly power over subordinate workers.
   b. A tendency to create Jerusalem centers near large institutions.
   c. The politicizing of appointments of ambitious workers.
   d. The difficulty to speak out against apostasy and sin in the church.
   e. An avenue through which apostasy, worldliness and blasphemous worship services have been introduced.
6. Dangers commonly found in lay ministries:

a. The development of ungodly independence.
   b. Competition among ministries for financial support.
   c. A fertile field for the spread of winds of doctrine.
   d. Exercising kingly power.
7 God calls for dedicated lay and denominational ministries to work in unity, in truth, and reghteousness.

Chapter 3

The Call to Lay and Self-Supporting Work

ONLY those who are prepared to devote their entire lives to Christ should consider entering lay or self-supporting work. Individuals who have been chosen of God to enter such work should do so, for it is a call to sacred ministry.

How can one know that he or she is chosen of God to accomplish such a divine work? This is a matter which has puzzled the minds of many Seventh-day Adventists. When Isaiah was called he was directly called to his self-supporting work by the voice of God.

> In the year that king Uzziah died I saw also the Lord sitting upon a throne, high and lifted up, and his train filled the temple. Above it stood the seraphims: each one had six wings; with twain he covered his face, and with twain he covered his feet, and with twain he did fly. And one cried unto another, and said, Holy, holy, holy, is the Lord of hosts: the whole earth is full of his glory. And the posts of the door moved at the voice of him that cried, and the house was filled with smoke. Then said I, Woe is me! For I am undone; because I am a man of unclean lips, and I dwell in the midst of a people of unclean lips: for mine eyes have seen the King, the Lord of hosts. Then flew one of the seraphims unto me, having a live coal in his hand, which he had taken with the tongs from off the altar: and he laid it upon my mouth, and said, Lo, this hath touched thy lips; and thine iniquity is taken away, and thy sin purged. Also

> I heard the voice of the Lord, saying, Whom shall I send, and who will go for us? Isaiah 6:1–8

Let us analyze this call step by step, for these are the steps we must follow.

1. Isaiah had, under God's grace, caught a glimpse of Christ in His temple where He mediates for His people (verse 1).
2. Isaiah witnessed evidence of the infinite holiness of God and the awe in which the angels adore the Majesty of heaven (verses 2–4).
3. Isaiah recognized his own utter unworthiness (verse 5, first part).
4. Isaiah's eyes were looking to Jesus (verse 5, last part).
5. Isaiah was free from sin (verses 6, 7).
6. Isaiah recognized God's call upon his service (verse 8, first part).

When each man or woman has fulfilled all these steps, that individual is chosen of God to enter service for Him. Without such a preparation no individual will receive a divine appointment.

Those preparing for God's service must first study the sanctuary service, for here is encapsulated the entire plan of salvation with Christ, our Redeemer and our High Priest, central to that salvation. It is this message which Christ commissions us to bear to the world.

We must worship our God in holiness, for all servants of God are free from sin—have confessed and, in the power of the Holy Spirit, forsaken all known sin—and are living holy lives which fit them for heaven. The privilege of service in the ranks of God is accorded by grace alone, to all who are fitted for heaven.

> But now being made free from sin, and become servants to God, ye have your fruit unto holiness, and the end everlasting life Romans 6:22

Reread Romans 6:22 above. This Scriptural passage provides

a crucial message for all who seek a place in God's service. It is also crucial to our personal salvation, for only genuine servants of God will receive the seal of the Living God.

> And I saw another angel ascending from the east, having the seal of the living God: and he cried with a loud voice to the four angels, to whom it was given to hurt the earth and the sea, Saying, Hurt not the earth, neither the sea, nor the trees, till we have sealed the servants of our God in their foreheads. Revelation 7:2, 3

There is no place for self-confidence in the hearts of those who seek the service of God, to be called of Him, for none is worthy. It is a great mystery that God has called sinners, albeit repented, to the holiest of duties—the task of delivering His last and greatest message of love to the one and only lost world.

It was not until Isaiah turned his eyes upon Jesus in His sanctuary that he recognized his undone condition and his desperate need to turn in full repentance to Christ.

> Did he [Isaiah] think himself unworthy before he had a view of God's glory?—No; he imagined himself in a righteous state before God.
> *Seventh-day Adventist Bible Commentary*, Vol. 4, 1139

How important it is for all men or women preparing for self-supporting or lay-work to turn their eyes to Jesus. The prophet Zechariah wrote prophetically,

> . . . they shall look upon me whom they have pierced.
> Zechariah 12:10

Paul, an example for every self-supporting worker, admonished us to look toward our Savior.

> For our conversation is in heaven; from whence also we look for the Saviour, the Lord Jesus Christ: Who shall change our vile body, that it may be fashioned like unto his glorious body, according to the working whereby he is able even to subdue all things unto himself.
> Philippians 3:20, 21

The Call to Lay and Self-Supporting Work

> So Christ was once offered to bear the sins of many, and unto them that look for him shall he appear the second time without sin unto salvation.   Hebrews 9:28

God can provide power to overcome sin for all who seek Him in love in preparation for service.

> If ye love me, keep my commandments.   John 14:15

> Now unto him that is able to keep you from falling, and to present you faultless before the presence of his glory with exceeding joy.   Jude 24

Only those who love Christ wholeheartedly will receive His recruitment to service. When an individual has committed his life unselfishly to Christ and received His redeeming power, he or she will "hear" the call of God to service. Only then does he truly respond as did Isaiah,

> Here am I; send me.   Isaiah 6:8, last part

If we have given ourselves in love to God's cause, then we are marshaled into His service. Of the more than 1,500,000,000 in this world who profess to serve God, all are called to service, but only a small number are selected by God, for

> Many be called, but few chosen.   Matthew 20:16

Why is this so? The reason is plain. Only a precious few follow the necessary steps cited above from the experience of Isaiah, in preparation for selection by God to enter His service. How may one know if God has chosen him or her to work for Him? We know when we have dedicated our whole soul to Christ's service in purity, by yielding to His will and His power.

> Put on therefore, as the elect [chosen] of God, holy and beloved, bowels of mercies, kindness, humbleness of mind, meekness, longsuffering.   Colossians 3:12

> But we are bound to give thanks alway to God for you, brethren beloved of the Lord, because God hath from the beginning chosen you to salvation through sanctification

of the Spirit and belief of the truth.
2 Thessalonians 2:13

Christ has encouraged us by His detailed creation of our very being. We must recognize that we are unique and special to Him and infinitely precious in His sight.

> I will praise thee; for I am fearfully and wonderfully made: marvellous are thy works; and that my soul knoweth right well. My substance was not hid from thee, when I was made in secret, and curiously wrought in the lowest parts of the earth. Thine eyes did see my substance, yet being unperfect; and in thy book all my members were written, which in continuance were fashioned, when as yet there was none of them. How precious also are thy thoughts unto me, O God! How great is the sum of them! If I should count them, they are more in number than the sand: when I awake, I am still with thee. Psalm 139:14–18

Remember that every part of us was fashioned by our Creator before our existence commenced. How encouraging is this knowledge!

God had chosen Isaiah prior to his birth.

> Thus saith the Lord that made thee, and formed thee from the womb, which will help thee. . . . Thus saith the Lord, thy redeemer, and he that formed thee from the womb, I am the Lord that maketh all things; that stretcheth forth the heavens alone; that spreadeth abroad the earth by myself.
> Isaiah 44:2, 24

> Listen, O isles, unto me; and hearken, ye people, from far; The Lord hath called me from the womb; from the bowels of my mother hath he made mention of my name.
> Isaiah, 49:1

Jeremiah was informed that God selected him for self-supporting work prior to his existence.

> Before I formed thee in the belly I knew thee; and before thou camest forth out of the womb I sanctified thee, and I ordained thee a prophet unto the nations.
> Jeremiah 1:5

The Call to Lay and Self-Supporting Work

God sanctified Jeremiah—set him aside for the holy mission of self-supporting work—before his birth. God has likewise set each one of us apart for the holy commission to take His gracious message of redemption worldwide. Whether we accept the commission and finally receive the call, is our choice. God has specially recorded all the details of each of us in the heavenly records. How precious we are to him! May we not hesitate to follow His calling.

> For thou hast possessed my reins: thou hast covered me in my mother's womb. I will praise thee; for I am fearfully and wonderfully made: marvellous are thy works; and that my soul knoweth right well, My substance was not hid from thee, when I was made in secret, and curiously wrought in the lowest parts of the earth. Thine eyes did see my substance, yet being unperfect; and in thy book all my members were written, which in continuance were fashioned, when as yet there was none of them.
> Psalm 139:13–16

Some God calls as lay-witnesses, others as workers in small self-supporting ministries and others in larger self-supporting ministries. But we are all called.

John the Baptist was called to self-supporting work even though he was of the priestly tribe of Levi. His father, Zacharias, was assured that—

> For he shall be great in the sight of the Lord, and shall drink neither wine nor strong drink; and he shall be filled with the Holy Ghost, even from his other's womb. And many of the children of Israel shall he turn to the Lord their God. And he shall go before him in the spirit and power of Elias, to turn the hearts of the fathers to the children, and the disobedient to the wisdom of the just, to make ready a people.
> Luke 1:15–17

Likewise, Ezekiel, the priest was called into self-supporting work. So today some ordained ministers are called into self-supporting work. The authors are part of a growing number who have responded to such a call.

Each Seventh-day Adventist before his or her birth has

been called to present the Elijah message, as was John the Baptist. God has provided each of us with a will to heed or reject this call. The use of our will determines our eligibility to enter the service of God.

We may be assured that God has prepared each of us to labor in His service even before we were conceived. Be assured He will choose us for service, whether it be in lay or self-supporting work, when we meet the requirements which God set forth for Isaiah. We do not dare enter such sacred work until God has fashioned us after His divine similitude, until we have chosen to serve Him with the whole heart. If we stumble and fall into sin after making this decision, do not retire from service, for our loving God has assured us:

> My little children, these things write I unto you, that ye sin not. And if any man sin, we have an advocate with the Father, Jesus Christ the righteous. 1 John 2:1

Yet it must be remembered that there are some sins so serious in their implications, sins which so dishonor God's church and His cause, that they demand church disfellowshipment. Such lay or self-supporting workers must step down from service until, by evidence of deep repentance and a regaining of their love for God and dedication to Him, they return to a life of virtue. We illustrate a few of these sins. Scripture teaches three basic grounds for disfellowshiping members:

1 Proclaiming heretical views.

> Holding faith, and a good conscience; which some having put away concerning faith have made shipwreck: of whom is Hymenaeus and Alexander; whom I have delivered unto Satan, that they may learn not to blaspheme.
> 1 Timothy 1:19, 20

> A man that is an heretick after the first and second admonition reject; knowing that he that is such is subverted, and sinneth, being condemned of himself. Titus 3:10, 11

2 Open, major sin.

> It is reported commonly that there is fornication among you, and such fornication as is not so much as named among the Gentiles, that one should have his father's wife. . . . In the name of our Lord Jesus Christ, when ye are gathered together, and my spirit, with the power of our Lord Jesus Christ, To deliver such an one unto Satan for the destruction of the flesh, that the spirit may be saved in the day of the Lord Jesus. Your glorying is not good. Know ye not that a little leaven leaveneth the whole lump? Purge out therefore the old leaven, that ye may be a new lump, as ye are unleavened. For even Christ our passover is sacrificed for us: . . . I wrote unto you in an epistle not to company with fornicators: . . . But now I have written unto you not to keep company, if any man that is called a brother be a fornicator, or covetous, or an idolater, or a railer, or a drunkard, or an extortioner; with such an one no not to eat. . . . But them that are without God judgeth. Therefore put away from among yourselves that wicked person. 1 Corinthians 5:1, 4–7, 9, 11, 13

3   Disorderly conduct.

> Now we command you, brethren, in the name of our Lord Jesus Christ, that ye withdraw yourselves from every brother that walketh disorderly, and not after the tradition which he received of us. 2 Thessalonians 3:6

Even when such individuals return to a life of virtue it is prudent that they no longer accept leadership roles, for their past major breach of faith, while claiming to follow Christ, disqualifies them. Self-supporting and lay workers must thus take great care daily to yield their lives to their Lord and seek His guidance and divine wisdom.

SUMMARY

1   Lessons from God's call to Isaiah:
   a. We must gain a glimpse of Jesus.
   b. We must capture the awe with which we approach God.

      c. We must recognize our own unworthiness.
      d. Our eyes must be focused upon Jesus
      e. Through the indwelling Christ we must be free from sin.
      f. We must discern God's calling in our lives.
      g. We must worship God in the beauty of holiness.
2. Other lessons to learn:
      a. We must seek fruit from our witness.
      b. We must distrust self.
      c. We must acknowledge and experience the power of God to provide protection from sin.
      d. Our lives must be free from selfish ambitions.
      e. We are all called but are chosen only when we are sanctified.
      f. If we fall, we must quickly seek the forgiveness and restitution of Christ.
3. Very serious departures from the Lord include,
      a. Sharing heretical views.
      b. Open major sins.
      c. Disorderly conduct.

Chapter 4

A Brief History of Self-Supporting Work

IN all God-ordained movements, self-supporting work preceded denominational work. The patriarchs were self-supporting workers who lived through both the antediluvian period and the early postdiluvian era up to the Egyptian enslavement.

> Amid the prevailing corruption, Methuselah, Noah, and many others labored to keep alive the knowledge of the true God and to stay the tide of moral evil.
> *Patriarchs and Prophets*, 92

During the exodus, however, God established denominational work for the first time. The tribe of Levi was appointed by God to serve as the priestly tribe.

> Bring the tribe of Levi near, and present them before Aaron the priest, that they may minister unto him. And they shall keep his charge, and the charge of the whole congregation before the tabernacle of the congregation, to do the service of the tabernacle. And they shall keep all the instruments of the tabernacle of the congregation, and the charge of the children of Israel, to do the service of the tabernacle.
> Numbers 3:6–8

Their livelihood was dependent upon the faithfulness of the Israelites in returning their tithe for the priests' support. However, the establishment of a denominationally supported priesthood did not eliminate the continued ministry of the self-supporting workers. While in nowise do we believe that the self-supporting work was limited to the prophets, nevertheless the prophets were the prominent self-supporting workers of Old Testament times. As far back as the seventh patriarch there was a prophet amongst God's people.

> And Enoch also, the seventh from Adam, prophesied of these, saying, Behold, the Lord cometh with ten thousands of his saints.   Jude 14

Moses, the leader of God's people, was a prophet. Whereas the denominational workers were limited to men—the priests—this was not true of the self-supporting workers as the Bible features a number of notable women, the prophetesses. These included Miriam, the sister of Moses (Exodus 15:20), Huldah (2 Kings 22:14), Deborah (Judges 4:4) and the daughters of Philip (Acts 21:9). Indeed, at many times in pre-Christian history the Lord depended not upon priests but upon prophets to maintain the integrity of God's people or to bring rebukes and judgments against the chosen ones of God.

However, there were those of the priestly tribe who became self-supporting prophets. Practical examples are Jeremiah and Ezekiel in the Old Testament, mighty prophets of God, and John the Baptist, the forerunner of Christ, in the New Testament. It will be recalled that John's father, Zacharias, was a priest and therefore of the tribe of Levi. Thus John the Baptist could have been a practicing priest, but God chose him to self-supporting work and Jesus said of him,

> Verily I say unto you, Among them that are born of women there hath not risen a greater than John the Baptist.
> Matthew 11:11

Christ did not choose priests to be His disciples. He chose laymen, humble laymen at that, to be His followers, His disciples and His apostles. All the apostles were self-supporting workers. Sister White clearly identifies Paul especially as a self-supporting worker.

> It was as a self-supporting missionary that the apostle Paul labored in spreading the knowledge of Christ throughout the world. While daily teaching the gospel in the great

A Brief History of Self-Supporting Work   25

cities of Asia and Europe, he wrought at the trade of a craftsman to sustain himself and his companions.

Ministry of Healing, 154

With the onward corruption of the priesthood of the Christian Church which developed into the Roman Catholic Church, God raised up self-supporting workers. The mighty Celtic missionaries, of which there have been few greater in the history of the world, were self-supporting workers. Beginning with the school in Iona, on the windswept west coast of Scotland, under the leadership of the Irish prince Columba (521–597), to the schools at Lindisfarne led by men and women such as Aiden, Caedmon, Hilda and Colman, young Christians were trained for missionary service. At these schools missionaries were educated to take the pure gospel, not only through the British Isles but to continental Europe.

The seven educational schools of Dinooth, established near the town of Bangor in northern Wales, were great training centers of self-supporting missionaries. The most famous of the graduates was Columbanus, an Irishman who took with him thirteen young men to the primeval forest of France and there began his first self-supporting ministry at Luxor. His ministry was not limited to ministering in France. He later labored in Germany, Austria and ended his ministry raising up the famous school at Bobbio in northern Italy.

The Waldensians were also powerful self-supporting missionaries who, like the Celts, sought to present the true gospel in contrast to the pagan intrusions into the Roman Catholic Church. Further, the Huguenots and Albigenses sought to share the gospel in the regions they occupied.

Again, at the time of the Reformation there were denominational men such as Luther, Melancthon, Calvin and Knox who were forced to serve as self-supporting workers. Nor should we forget the staunch Anabaptists, many of whom were martyred for their faithfulness to Christ.

The Seventh-day Adventist Church began with self-supporting workers. There were no trained ministers in the beginning of the movement, although in the pre-1844 advent movement a number of well-known ministers joined with the laity to spread the message of the soon coming of Jesus Christ. Most famous of these were Baptist preacher William Miller and Presbyterian minister Charles Fitch. However, it was some years before those who became the leaders in the Seventh-day Adventist denomination were ordained and supported as full-time ministers of the gospel.

The work of the Seventh-day Adventist Church on every continent was begun by self-supporting workers. The first authenticated Seventh-day Adventist preacher was Fredrick Wheeler, who accepted the Sabbath message in 1844 in Washington, New Hampshire. In North America, others, such as Captain Joseph Bates, the Farnsworth brothers, and James and Ellen White were soon convicted of the Sabbath message. Young men, including Uriah Smith and John Andrews, pressed forward the advent message as laymen before being ordained as ministers.

The first continent outside North America to hear the Seventh-day Adventist message was Africa. Hannah More (1808–1868), an American missionary in Liberia heard the advent message in the early 1860s in New England before returning to her mission post at an orphanage in Liberia where she presented the Sabbath message. Soon, however, that message was rejected and she returned to the United States where she died in upstate Michigan.

The third continent to hear the Seventh-day Adventist message was Australia for, while Hannah More was teaching the Sabbath truth in Liberia, an Australian from Melbourne by the name of Alexander Dickson had visited this remote mission post and had accepted the Sabbath truth which Hannah More had shared with him. He brought the truth back to the city of Melbourne and scattered tracts on the Sabbath in 1864 more than two decades before the first denominational missionaries led by Elder Stephen Nelson Haskell (1833–1922) arrived to forward the gospel in the South Pacific.

The fourth continent to receive the gospel message was Europe, when the former Polish priest, then a Seventh-day

A Brief History of Self-Supporting Work 27

Adventist layman, Michael Belina Czechowski (1818–1876) took the gospel to northern Italy in 1864, and Switzerland in 1867.

The fifth continent to hear the message was Asia, when Abram La Rue (1822–1903) left America for Hong Kong when he had been rejected by the General Conference as a denominational worker. He spread the Seventh-day Adventist message far and wide after his arrival in 1888.

The last continent to hear the Seventh-day Adventist message was South America. This message was first preached and taught in Argentina by four German families who migrated from Russia to Kansas, where they had accepted the Seventh-day Adventist faith, and later immigrated to Argentina. There they presented the everlasting gospel message to some of the inhabitants of this southern continent. These few families appeared to be led by Jorge Riffel who had visited Argentina before settling in Kansas.

However, God also raised up denominational workers, ordained credentialed pastors, teachers, Bible workers, colporteurs and health workers. So it is today that God in His wisdom has appointed both denominational and self-supporting workers. It is God's desire that each arm of His work labor in the unity of truth and righteousness with one cooperative goal—to take the everlasting gospel to every nation, kindred, tongue and people, to share the hope of the soon return of a risen and high-priestly ministering Savior.

SUMMARY

1 God's work consistently began with self-supporting workers.
   a. The patriarchal leaders preceded the priesthood by about two thousand five hundred years.
   b. The prophets were the self-supporting workers of Old Testament times.
   c. Self-supporting apostles preceded the appointment of priests in the Christian church.
   d. All continents received the three angels' messages

from self-supporting workers before denominational missionaries arrived.
   - e. Denominationally appointed workers did not replace the need for self-supporting workers; for all members are called to God's service.
2. Self-supporting workers were often chosen of God to bring enlightenment and rebuke.
3. In the Dark and Middle Ages, God had self-supporting missionaries—the Waldensians, the Celts, Huguenots, Albigenses and Anabaptists.
4. The pre-1844 Advent Movement was largely a lay movement.
5. All continents received the three angels' messages first from lay workers.
   - a. 1844—Frederick Wheeler, New Hampshire, North America.
   - b. 1863—Hannah More, Liberia, Africa.
   - c. 1864—Alexander Dickson, Melbourne, Australia.
   - d. 1864—Michael Czechowski, Italy, Europe.
   - e. 1888—Abram La Rue, Hong Kong, Asia.
   - f. 1890—Jorge Riffel, Argentina, South America.

Chapter 5

Sensing a Need

MOST lay and self-supporting workers whom we have met have a vision and a focus to fulfill a special role in the hastening of the coming of the Lord. Most of these workers willingly sacrifice to further the cause of Christ. Lay and self-supporting ministries have exploded over the last twenty-five years. There are many hundreds of such ministries in the United States alone and, whereas twenty-five years ago outside the United States there were scarcely any self-supporting ministries, today every continent has a rapidly increasing number of lay ministries.

Our personal experience is a classical example. Until 1968 we had not so much as heard of self-supporting work. Thus we could never have envisaged serving in such a capacity. Colin was then the Chairman of the Education Department at Avondale College. Russell was serving the denomination as a physician at Penang Adventist Hospital, Malaysia. Colin's awareness of self-supporting work came only when a student at the college brought to him a small brochure of Wildwood Institute in Georgia. Like so many others, Colin's first reaction was this must be an off-shoot movement.

However, as under the urging of the student he read the brochure, he realized that Wildwood Institution did not fit the classical criteria of an off-shoot movement. Indeed, it seemed to be thoroughly Seventh-day Adventist and thoroughly loyal to both the truths and the practices of the Seventh-day Adventist Church. There was no hint of any schismatic or hostile reaction to the Seventh-day Adventist Church. Neither did the brochure suggest that the institution was offering new, startling "light" to add to or replace the tried and true pillars of the Seventh-day Adventist faith.

This introduction to self-supporting ministry was amazing to Colin. He shared it in correspondence with Russell. He had read through the nine volumes of the *Testimonies to the Church,* which on a number of occasions address the self-supporting work, yet the whole concept of self-supporting work escaped his attention. Colin first visited Wildwood in 1972 when he was serving as President of West Indies College (now Northern Caribbean University). Later, while President of Columbia Union College in Maryland, Colin twice visited Wildwood and returned with a profound admiration for the men and women who were serving there. He developed a special admiration for Elder William Frazee, the founder and "patriarch" of that institution. But never did either of the authors contemplate the thought of ministering in self-supporting work. It was one thing to admire this work, quite another to join it. After all we both were ordained to the gospel ministry of the Seventh-day Adventist Church, Colin in 1971, and Russell in 1980. We believed God called us into His ministry against our own years of resistance to the Holy Spirit's leading. Once we followed God's calling our focus was to contribute to the work to which God had called us through the denominational arm of the church. From that time forward we had taken the position that we would follow the calls of the Lord. We determined that it was not for us to forge the direction of our lives. Thus we waited upon God and therefore every call received we accepted.

There were times when there was confusion. For example when Colin was completing his studies at the University of Sydney he had two strong inquiries, one from Avondale College the other from the Southern Asian Division to serve as the principal of a large academy in India. His wife, Cheryl, and he favored the latter call. But once again they placed the situation before the Lord in prayer asking Him to make it plain where they should serve. The Lord did this quickly for the call to India closed up when it was learned that Colin could not be there for September, 1964 school opening, for

Sensing a Need

he had teaching obligations at the University of Sydney until the end of 1964.

Another situation occurred when Colin had completed his service as President of West Indies College in Jamaica. He received news of three calls which he was assured were coming to him: from Columbia Union College; Andrews University, and Loma Linda University. Colin favored Andrews University, his wife favored Loma Linda University. However they left the decision in the hands of the Lord asking Him to lead Colin to the institution where he should serve. Colin told the Lord that he would accept the first official call which actually reached him. To his surprise that call came from Columbia Union College. The official call to the post of Professor of Education at Andrews University was voted the same day but was sent by letter. The Columbia Union College call came the same day in a telephone call from Dr. George Akers, President of Columbia Union College.

There were other times when calls were placed for him. For example, when he was serving as Chairman of the Education Department at Avondale College, a call came for him to be the foundation principal of the newly established Sonoma College in Papua New Guinea. That call was blocked by the Avondale College principal. While serving at West Indies College, two calls were received, one to serve as Chairman of the Psychology Department at Southern Missionary College (now Southern Adventist University) and the other to serve as President of Caribbean Union College in Trinidad. Once again both those calls were blocked by the Inter-American Division leadership. While serving as President of Columbia Union College Colin was invited to accept the appointment to serve as the Educational Director of the Canadian Union Conference, but again that call was blocked. Still later, a call from Andrews University to be part of the doctoral program in Educational Psychology was also blocked once more by the Columbia Union.

It was this commitment to following the direction of the Lord which led us into self-supporting work. We doubt that we have discovered anyone who had such plain and unequivocal calls into self-supporting work. Neither of us would have chosen it, but God did and we believe that all who take up the responsibilities of self-supporting work should be assured that they have a call from God.

In Colin's situation, the issue which arose and eventually led to Colin entering self-supporting work was whether or not to relocate Columbia Union College to the countryside. In 1978, the latest of five efforts was made to move that college out of suburbia into a rural location consistent with the plain counsels of the Lord. Previous attempts had been made in 1921, 1956, 1964 and 1976. In 1978, by a narrow margin, it was voted to reject the proposal to move Columbia Union College to a rural environment. Colin knew this was directly contrary to the counsel of the Lord and therefore he prayed a prayer which he shared with no one, not even his wife, Cheryl. In that prayer Colin petitioned God that if the Lord saw it best for him to stay at Columbia Union College he would trust the Lord to give him the strength to carry on. His prayer continued along the lines that if God had somewhere Colin could serve Him more effectively, he would take whatever call came to him. Colin's mind, of course, was directed solely towards denominational work.

This direction was changed when soon after he had prayed that prayer Colin was called by the newly established Weimar Institute in northern California to serve as the inaugural Dean of the planned college. Shocked by receiving the call to an Institution in the self-supporting arm of the Lord's work, he immediately knew it to be God's will and accepted even though the initial stipend was ten dollars a week plus lodging.

The fact that Colin had known of a certainty that God called him into self-supporting work has been one of the greatest sustaining principles in his more than a quarter of a century of self-supporting work. It has been the most difficult, the most trying period of his life. But it has also been, by far, the most rewarding segment of his service for the Lord. His faith and trust in God has grown as has his gratitude to Him and love for Him. It has been a most fulfilling, growing experience. To have the assurance that God is leading one's ministry is a great consolation when facing difficulties or opposition.

The great proliferation of self-supporting ministries, we are convinced, is in the plan of God. The Lord is seeking to ignite the resources and fervor of the laity of the church to take the gospel to the world. Only when the vast army of laity sense the divine calling which God has placed upon their lives and service will the gospel advance with the might and scope which will take the three angels' messages to every nook and cranny of this world, reaching to every inhabitant.

> And he said unto them, Go ye into all the world, and preach the gospel to every creature.   Mark 16:15

Russell's experience in trusting God's guidance in his work has been no less faith-enhancing than Colin's, as he was awarded an Australian Commonwealth Government Scholarship to study medicine *after* the Government had gazetted the end of such scholarships. It would have been impossible to afford to study medicine at Sydney University had it not been for the payment of all fees for the six-year course and the provision of a stipend. There was no requirement to return the Government means expended after graduation. This freed Russell from any financial restraint which would have hindered him from accepting any successive calls to denominational mission service. God also guided Russell in a wonderful manner into self-supporting work. His has been a life well worth the living. Both of us look back on our lives and conclude that we would never choose to have lived our lives in any other manner than the one which God designed for us.

In modern times, self-supporting work had its origin in the poverty-stricken parts of southeastern United States. It began in sacrifice as people saw the need to spread the gospel rapidly and widely in locations where funds were available to support but few denominational workers. However, Sister White in no way limited self-supporting work to the poverty-stricken South. She urged that self-supporting workers go into the large cities of the world.

> God calls upon his people to awake. There is much work to do, and no one is to say, "We do not want this one. He will stand in our way. He will hinder us." Can not God take care of that? Are there not those in this congregation who will settle in London to work for the Master? Are there not those who will go to the great city as self-supporting missionaries? But while missionaries are to do all they can to be self-supporting, let those who remain here, who Sabbath after Sabbath come to the Tabernacle to hear the word of God, who have every convenience and advantage, let them beware how they say to those they send to foreign fields, destitute of every facility and advantage, "You must be self-supporting."
> *General Conference Bulletin*, April 22, 1901

> The European field must receive the attention it must have. And we are not to forget the needy fields close at hand. Look at New York! What representation for the truth is there in that city. How much help has been sent there? Our education and health work must be established there, and this work must be given financial aid till it is self-supporting.
> *General Conference Bulletin*, April 22, 1901

We know that during the closing scenes of earth's history spirit-filled men and women will be hastening door to door to spread the gospel. We also know that not all will be men and women trained in literary institutions.

> Under the showers of the latter rain the inventions of man, the human machinery, will at times be swept away, the boundary of man's authority will be as broken reeds, and the Holy Spirit will speak through the living, human agent, with convincing power. No one then will watch to see if the sentences are well rounded off, if the grammar is faultless.
> *Selected Messages*, Book. 2, 58–59

The need for self-supporting workers is urgent. The work force must multiply greatly in order to take the gospel to the world. This handbook is designed to help the dedicated laymen and women to shoulder responsibilities to which God is calling all those who have been baptized into the life and ministry of Jesus Christ.

SUMMARY

1. Self-supporting workers must have a clear calling and vision from the Lord.
2. Self-supporting workers must possess a willingness to serve in self-sacrifice.
3. Self-supporting workers should never contemplate an attitude of seeking to present startling or speculative concepts as new light.
4. Listen only to the calls from the Lord.
5. There is a rapid increase of self-supporting ministries world-wide in preparation for laity to play their rightful role in hastening the coming of Jesus.

Chapter 6

Single Focused Self-Supporting Work

HARTLAND Institute and Remnant Ministries, where the authors have the privilege to serve, are multi-phase self-supporting organizations. However, many self-supporting institutions concentrate their work upon a single primary focus. The most common single ministry focus is in the area of health. This is understandable because we know that the very last work which will be accomplished before the close of human probation will be the medical missionary work. It is important for those who undertake this work to make it a strong soul-winning ministry. To neglect the conversion of souls would be to ignore the healthiest measure in the world—eternal life. Otherwise they limit themselves to excellent health education while failing to use the medical and health work as an avenue to open the minds of men and women to the things of God. A work ignoring the conversion of souls is no ministry at all.

The health work may take many different forms. For example, some have trained in the use of natural remedies, following carefully the instruction and guidance to be found in the Spirit of Prophecy. This provides special opportunities to work with the affluent and the influential in society. Frequently there is no other successful avenue by which such people will be receptive to the gospel. However, the health message should be made available to all strata of society for most people are interested in health issues, especially those who are aware that they have serious health problems.

It has been our experience, however, that the poorer the people are, as a general rule, the less interested they are in health practices. This is true in western countries as well as developing nations. The health work can take many different forms. Some have successfully established hydrotherapy and massage treatment centers with great success. Others have opened vegan restaurants and/or health food stores. Still others have established health-counseling services or minister through cooking schools and stop-smoking clinics. Others have adopted the difficult task of working with drug addicts including alcoholics. Still others minister to those with emotional illnesses. Some have opened facilities where they offer a range of health services on an out-patient basis. Others have established health and wellness centers which provide live-in facilities. The scope, the size and the cost outlay can vary greatly. Some of these ministries will be operated by a single individual or a family, while others will be of such a scope that a significant staff is involved which may include physicians, nurses, physical therapists, hydrotherapists, massage therapists, exercise physiologists, dieticians and nutritional specialists. The field is as broad or as narrow as is the size of the operation.

Many have carried forward such successful ministries from their homes. Others have built much more elaborate facilities depending upon the goals and objectives which they have and the finances which are available. Some have begun small but under the blessing of God have increased as the opportunity permitted.

Then there is the personal ministries form of self-supporting work. One of the most effective and the least costly to establish is the colporteur ministry where the successful colporteur may sell truth-filled literature door to door. Sometimes the entire family is engaged in the activity. This situation not only permits the opportunity to place precious truth in the hearts and minds of the purchasers but also provides an income to support fully or in part the needs of the colporteur and his family.

Another inexpensive individual ministry is Bible work. We have been greatly impressed, for example, at the individual work of young and old in Auckland, New Zealand. We were especially inspired by a young lady, Elizabeth Aratai. Elizabeth is of Cook Island descent and is a fervent door-to-door worker seeking those who will respond to her invitation to Bible studies. Already she has brought a number of souls into the Seventh-day Adventist faith and, on one occasion when we were visiting and preaching in Auckland, she had twelve separate Bible studies a week with individuals and families. Some of those Bible study contacts attended the camp meeting and have expressed their great blessing from the messages they heard. Some have gone forth in baptism.

It is not difficult to find Bible study contacts. Yes, in some places it will be more difficult than others. Yet the methodology is the same. It is a simple matter of knocking on doors until someone responds to the invitation to study the Bible. While we realize that in the southern United States, the Bible belt, it is much easier to gain Bible study interests than in many other parts of the world, yet in any religiously free country the same procedures can succeed. Colin recalls challenging a class of twenty-eight students at Hartland to find one house open to Bible study. He asked the students to keep a record as to the number of doors they had knocked upon before they received a positive response to the invitation. The greatest number of door-knocks it took any student to gain a Bible study was seven. Four of the students were successful at the very first home. However, it is much more rewarding if we follow the Bible principle of working two by two. Those who are experienced and skilled in Bible studies can accomplish great success by taking with them a younger or less experienced person so that they might train their companion. Later, the ones trained can develop into successful trainers of others. Thus the work expands.

The beauty of such ministry is that it can be undertaken in the discretionary time which we have available. We must keep in mind that it is not too long ago that employees worked forty-four hours a week and a century ago it was usually forty-eight hours a week. Those additional hours provide for us the opportunity to accomplish something special for the Lord. Sadly, today much of that discretionary time is flitted away either in front of the television set or the Internet screen or in idle sports and entertainment. What we do with our discretionary time is a reliable barometer of our dedication to God and our burden for souls.

There are other soul-winning endeavors which cost little except earnest use of time and effort. The ministry for the needy, the elderly, the infirm and the sick are avenues for these endeavors. Working for such souls fulfills the words of Jesus in Matthew 25:31–46 where Christ exhorted us to feed and water the hungry and thirsty, to visit the sick and those in prison, clothe the naked, showing a burden for those who are in desperate need.

One of the most effective ministries is the prison ministry. This is an all-too-often neglected work. Many a poor soul in prison, often cut off from friends and family, is hungering for hope and the understanding of how to break from those sins which have led him into the prison system. Some are left without hope in this world, especially in countries like the United States, where so many felons are sentenced to serve out the rest of their natural life in prison. They may have no future in this life, but we can bring to them the glorious opportunity that Christ offers for a life of eternal freedom from sin, freedom from incarceration and freedom from the frequent threats which are often a part of prison life.

Nursing homes also offer a fruitful field of ministry. Often at the end of life, especially after the loss of a life partner, lonely souls are seeking encouragement. This is a work that can, in the sunset years of life, present hope and bring salvation to saddened and neglected individuals. It is especially important to involve children and youth in this ministry. The elderly usually respond well to the ministry of the young.

It is possible for even the elderly and the infirm to minister to others. We offer two examples. Colin and his wife Cheryl visited in Kressville, the hospital section of the large Seventh-day Adventist retirement center at Cooranbong near Avondale College in Australia, a woman whom they had known for many years. This lady at the time was ninety-eight years of age and bed-ridden. We were surprised as we entered the room to see her propped up in bed diligently undertaking crochet work. Of course it did not take us long to ask what she had in mind with her crocheting. We knew that she probably had to forfeit her government pension to help pay for the cost of her hospitalization. Naturally we wondered if she was seeking to earn a little money to give her some discretionary means to spend. We soon discovered that was not her goal. Her whole goal was to continue what had been her lifetime habit of sending funds to the South Pacific Mission Field. She was making doilies and runners and even tablecloths with a deftness and skill which was nothing short of remarkable for a woman of her age. Obviously we could not leave her without buying a number of the items which she had already completed.

Then there was Pastor Korinth in Berlin, Germany. Pastor Korinth, a retired minister who had served through both Nazi and Communist oppression in East Germany, could not cease working for souls though well into his eighties. At first in his retirement, he distributed much literature. By the time we met him a second time, his legs were failing and to continue that ministry was no longer possible. However he found an alternative way to spread the word through telephone ministry. He simply dialed telephone numbers systematically, numbers in the Berlin telephone book, and in this way sought to introduce Christ to all who were interested. He was not deterred when he received rude or unresponsive replies to his calls but continued daily to call these strangers, noting those who responded favorably, and setting up regular contacts with some of these precious souls.

There are other lay people who have commenced radio programs, funding them themselves or, in some cases, receiving help from fellow church members. Some of these programs have been straightforward preaching on present-truth themes. Others have occupied a short time in preaching followed by question and answer sessions for the listening public. Such a ministry is run in the Asheville area of North Carolina by Elder Clark Floyd and Brother Lee Forbes. Of course there is always the opportunity to offer literature either free or at a price or simply for a donation.

There are other remarkable ways which require only effort and earnest dedication. The Internet, for example, has opened up a vast opportunity to share the gospel with whomever may read it. Those in English speaking countries have a great opportunity, for by far the largest number of Internet users around the world have English as either their first or second language. As we write this book, more than two hundred million people have access to the Internet in English and the number is rapidly growing. This is a marvelous field for service before an audience of huge magnitude.

All Christians, able-bodied and clear in mind, can find a mission field if they have the dedication. It can be in any of the areas above or it may be a mission in seeking the backslidden Seventh-day Adventists, many of whom may have left the church but in their heart of hearts they still know that the Seventh-day Adventist message is God's last message. It is not uncommon that all such individuals need is someone to show an interest in them, to encourage them. Some do not need study so much as they need to be assured that the fellowship of Jesus is witnessed in the fellowship of loving and growing Christians. The opportunities are open for all, even some who are seriously incapacitated, to show that they love the Lord more than anything else in the world, and while ever He sustains them they are able to work for the salvation of souls.

Even many who have been well trained in the service of God may choose to do part-time self-supporting work. This is why it is so important for every Christian to learn a trade or an income-generating occupation.

Some who choose self-sacrificing, self-supporting work can take up a trade in their home or shed or in any simple structure to engage in manufacturing or packaging, where with earnestness they, and other family members can work diligently in the morning, maybe into the early afternoon, and then do the work of God in the latter part of the day. The greatest hindrances to ministry are—

1 becoming involved so fully in earthly pursuits that there is no time for ministry;
2 in convincing ourselves that we lack the training or the skills to be faithful missionary workers.

Remember the words of the hymn, "There's a work for Jesus none but you can do."

The options for ministry are so many that there will be one for you. What about preparing tracts, preparing audio- or video-tapes or even CDs and DVDs? Tapes, CDs, Videos and DVDs can also be broadcast on the world-wide web.

Most can distribute truth filled literature. Let us recommend the *Last Generation* magazine for adults and *Young Disciple* for youth. Can you imagine what would happen if every Seventh-day Adventist had a personal ministry?

We and other members of our family would not likely be Seventh-day Adventists today if it were not for the fervent efforts of lay people in sharing the gospel message. In 1899, our maternal grandmother found a religious tract in her letter-box. She was a very devout member of the Primitive Methodist Church who loved the Lord and believed fully in the Words of Scripture. In the following two weeks, on the same morning of the week, she found further tracts in her letter-box. Reading them she was very impressed with what she had read and was anxious to discover who was placing these tracts in her box the night before. Thus she decided a week later that on the night before she would expect to find another tract in her box, she would stand by the screen door close to the street where her letter-box was located. Eventually in the dim, gas lights of that era she perceived a shadowy figure inserting material in letter-boxes further up the street. As soon as the individual approached her house she quickly moved out and discovered a seventeen-year-old youth as the one who had been making these weekly distributions.

He was a shy young man but he possessed sufficient presence of mind to ask our grandmother, after she had said she was enjoying these tracts, whether she would be interested in having Bible studies with a lady Bible worker. Our grandmother enthusiastically accepted the opportunity and the rest is history. In 1900, she was baptized into the Seventh-day Adventist faith in the city of Newcastle, Australia. Pastor Imery, for later this youth became an ordained minister of the Seventh-day Adventist Church, began his search for souls in his teen-age years. We had the privilege to hear him preach when we were lads about seven or eight years of age in the very early 1940s.

In 1915, a layman, Brother Bachhaus, a German, came to the Barossa Valley of South Australia about fifty miles north of the capital city of Adelaide. The Barossa Valley had been settled by German immigration from the 1840s. Our great-grandfather, Samuel David Standish, was a deacon in the Reformed Lutheran Church in the small town of Tanunda.

Like our maternal grandmother, our great-grandfather was a man of deep piety who needed only to understand the Scriptures to accept the Sabbath truth and the Seventh-day Adventist faith. The work of Brother Bachhaus was fruitful and quite a number of German families, some of which, over the years, have given life-long service to the work of God, not only in the South Pacific area, but a number of places overseas, joined the church.

It is not only the souls which are brought into the kingdom who are your reward, but, if properly trained and instructed, these souls have the potential to bring other members of their own families and of the community into the fellowship of Jesus Christ. It is like the stone thrown into the pond which creates a ripple which continues to expand from the initial point of impact. So the conversion of one soul may lead to a continuing impact as other souls are led to the Lord. The result of ones' witness may continue until the close of human probation.

In our own experience, our father had persisted in seeking Bible study contacts. About the age of twelve we continued to put pressure on our father to permit us to join him in his Bible studies. We were fascinated by the stories and reports he brought back after each Bible study. Eventually our Dad agreed, with very strict rules, for us to visit one of his Bible studies. Our role was simply to open up the texts and silently read them as our father presented the Bible study. Somehow we felt part of the ministry. We had been engaged in the annual Harvest Ingathering Campaign each year and during what was then called "Big Week," a week when a special book was sold around the community to the public. We had also been involved with some visitation of the sick with our family. Each year we were involved in distributing advertising for crusades. While students at Avondale College, weekly we were involved in branch Sabbath school work on Sabbath afternoons.

However, it was as an eighteen-year-old, when Colin had been appointed teacher to his first school in a remote country area of Australia called Ophir Glen on the north coast of New South Wales, that his vision for soul saving was expanded. A twenty-one-year-old man, John Wilkerson, was so happy to have another young man in the church, he invited Colin to join with him to visit his four Bible-study contacts every Sabbath afternoon. Quickly Colin realized that none of the four families with whom John was studying in this rural community was the least bit interested, although they were pleasant and they were hospitable. Colin wondered why John, an Englishman by birth, could not see that the people had little interest in the Bible studies. However, Colin continued to accompany John until eventually John asked if Colin would present the studies the next week, to which he assented. Colin found the responses to his studies no better than they had been to John's.

It was with a sense of relief to Colin when two or three weeks later John said, "You know, Colin, I don't think these people are interested." Colin thought that would be the end of their mission enterprise. John, however, was too committed to the Lord to cease these activities. He simply said, "Why don't we go down to Cudgen Headlands next week and see if we can find some new interests?" With minimum enthusiasm Colin assented to that invitation and the next Sabbath they traveled to do door-to-door work. Colin had never been there before and was surprised to see how few people lived in Cudgen Headlands. There was a scattering of houses on both sides of the road which extended for a mile or so, often with significant distances between houses. Probably not more than thirty or forty homes made up this little community.

After Colin had been distributing literature on the right-hand side and was nearly three-quarters of the way to the end of his side of the road, he realized that there had been no sign of John for some time. He clearly had not left the first house. Colin wondered how many of the homes on the left-hand side he would have to visit. Eventually John came out of the first home and began to run towards him. Colin stopped and started to walk back towards John. By the time John reached Colin, he was out of breath but he urged Colin to return to this first home because he had found people who were enthusiastic about his visit. Of course, they went back to the home. There was an elderly couple in their early seventies. Before they left the house that day Colin was just as enthusiastic as John. These people had been seeking to understand the words of Scripture for many years. Before John and Colin left, this couple said, "Young men, we have waited a lifetime to hear the things you are telling us today. Will you come back again next week?" Of course, with great enthusiasm John and Colin assured them that they would be back. Before John and Colin departed, the couple asked if it were possible to invite others to the meeting the next week. They eagerly assented to the request and could not wait for the next Sabbath afternoon.

To their shock, when John and Colin arrived at the couple's old-fashioned Australian, home there were over thirty people in the large lounge room. After a week or two they said, "We would like to sing hymns. Is there any way you can bring a piano or an organ?" They said they would do their best. The couple explained that there was a woman in the community who could play either the organ or the piano and they would invite her to come.

Early the next week Colin contacted the North New South Wales Conference office more than five hundred miles to the south. Colin was told that the Conference had a little pump organ which they would gladly send to them by train. And so the next week they, with a number of other folk from Ophir Glen, took the pump organ and there was much hymn singing.

What wonderful meetings they continued to have. You can imagine their joy at the first baptism many months later when eight precious souls, including the couple we had first contacted and the woman who had come to play the organ, were baptized into the fellowship of God's church and His kingdom. But that was not to be the end. A significant number of others were baptized from that little community close to the Pacific Ocean in that subtropical region of Australia.

The story did not end there. Many years later, when Colin was chairman of the Education Department at Avondale College, he was registering students when an eighteen-year-old young lady came to register. Asked for her name, she responded, "Diane Rabjones." While the name Jones is a very common name, Colin had only heard the surname "Rabjones" at Cudgen Headlands. This was the name of the elderly couple who had responded so wonderfully sixteen years before to the message of God. Naturally Colin was intrigued by her name and asked her from where she came. She responded by saying, "Well, it is such a tiny place on the far north coast of New South Wales that you probably would not have heard of it." Before she had said any more Colin said, "You come from Cudgen Headlands." She was amazed that he would know of such a tiny village. When John and Colin had studied with the family sixteen years before, Diane was the two-year-old granddaughter who was brought by the Rabjones's daughter-in-law conscientiously every week to the meetings. Now she was enrolling at Avondale College committed to train for the service of the Lord. We can never know the full extent of our ministry until we reach the kingdom of heaven.

SUMMARY

1. Below is a list of ministries which individuals and families may undertake in their discretionary time, most of which can be conducted from, or in their homes, at little cost.
    a. Simple community health work using God's special therapies.
    b. Hydrotherapy or massage.
    c. Cooking schools.
    d. Stop-smoking clinics.
    e. Drug rehabilitation.
    f. Nutritional seminars.
    g. Exercise instruction.
    h. Correspondence Bible school.
    i. Door to door Bible work.
    j. Prison ministry.
    k. Nursing home visitation.
    l. Visitation of elderly who are confined to their homes.
    m. Telephone ministry.
    n. Audio- and video-tape ministry as well as CD and DVD ministry.
    o. Web-site evangelism.

Single Fucused Self-Supporting Work 47

- p. Door to door literature distribution.
- q. It is also possible to have a radio and maybe television program prepared at home for local radio or television broadcasts or to be aired on the world-wide web.

Chapter 7

Individual and Family Self-Supporting Work

OFTEN we think of self-supporting ministry as primarily associated with institutions. However, in reality only a small percentage of self-supporting workers are found in sizable institutions. For example, it was said that more than one hundred and fifty self-supporting units were spawned during the sixty-year history of Madison Institution in Tennessee. However, many of these self-supporting initiatives were individual or family units, sometimes with one or two non-family members assisting. While there is an important place for larger institutions, nevertheless, the vast majority of lay work will, by its nature, be developed by individuals or families. Indeed, to follow the counsel of the Lord, every Seventh-day Adventist family should be carrying on a vigorous and active self-supporting ministry. There are tremendous advantages in this program. Above all a home self-supporting ministry can be operated with minimal operating and overhead costs. After all, the individual or family already lives in a home and often all it takes to set up such a ministry is to put aside one room or a shed to launch and operate the work of the ministry. Such a ministry can be operated in many avenues, as will be witnessed from the examples below.

We think of the ministry of Jonathan Bennett in Leicestershire in England. As a teenager, Jonathan developed a vision to distribute truth-filled literature to the approximately twenty million homes in Great Britain. He, with the assistance of his family and, from time to time, some friends, has already contacted millions of those homes and he is determined to continue to reach out to the others. He dreamed big and God is honoring that dream.

Also in England is Reggie Wright, a former Hartland student, born to a West Indian immigrant family, who, in spite of battling sickle-cell anemia, is doing a mighty work in evangelism with the assistance of close colleagues. Then there is Norman Hopkins who has a ministry which frequently takes him to Romania and some other countries of continental Europe. Gordon and Heather Anderson have a fine correspondence Bible study program which reaches out to large numbers of families in Great Britain.

An excellent tape ministry and home church are operated by Roger and Jean Rose from their home in Norwich, England. The home and grounds of Richard and Laura Humphries, in the little village of Gazeley in Suffolk, England, has been opened for camp meetings five times annually for almost two decades. Adam Ramdin from England, a Hartland graduate, has a successful ministry as an intercontinental evangelist.

In Australia, Glynn Harnell from Queensland, inspired by Jonathan Bennett, is doing a similar work in the state in which he lives. Glynn is a taxi driver by occupation. Already he has distributed literature to large segments of his home state, Queensland, and to some towns of New South Wales. Robert Pannekoek, a Hartland graduate, is providing a fine health and evangelism ministry in many parts of the world from his home base in Taree, Australia. Rod Bailey has been blessed in conducting a successful health education center in southwestern West Australia.

Glynn's parents, Lucy and the late Morris Harnell, have conducted Australia's oldest continuing ministry from their home. They have organized an annual camp meeting in Brisbane and the ALMA (Adventist Lay Members Action) meetings uplifting truth on a regular basis throughout the year. They also commenced a book ministry. Since Morris' death in 1999, Sister Harnell, now beyond her eightieth birthday, ably continues this work.

Ula and Ron Cable have operated *The Anchor* magazine. This is a ministry of warning and encouragement to God's people. Their magazine is distributed world-wide. Ula's skills in proofreading and her wise counsel, and both Ron and Ula's skills in research have greatly benefited numerous other ministries. Dr. Barry Harker has developed a distance learning Christian training program through the Internet from his home in Southern Queensland. Walter Langaneckert, a Hartland graduate and former staff, and family, have a health and training program also in Southern Queensland.

A number of Australian pastors, retired from denominational service, conduct active preaching ministries, aided by their wives. These include Pastors Austin Cooke, Maurice Peterson, Frank Saunders, Thomas Turner, William Turner, and Desmond Williams.

In West Malaysia, Pastor Joseph David conducts a ministry from his home which meets the needs of faithful, searching souls throughout Peninsular Malaysia.

The Janek family in the Czech Republic minister through their health food stores. Olga Brabcova, her family and some friends, are doing a mighty ministry in witnessing through health seminars and cooking schools, and now in translating, printing and distributing Ellen White Comments on the Sabbath School Lessons. The Nommik family in Estonia has undertaken evangelistic work. The father is a retired minister and the ministry is largely carried on by two of his sons, Viktor, a faithful Seventh-day Adventist minister who is now involved in self-supporting work, and his school teacher brother, Villi. They have conducted a number of successful crusades in their home city of Johve and in surrounding areas. Viktor supports himself and family with his skills in the building trade; Villi is an English teacher. Jay Krueger (from North Dakota), a Hartland graduate, is engaged in soul-winning ministry in Sweden.

On the east coast of South Africa, the DeBeer family, Elwyn and Dorothy, are conducting a vigorous literature and soul winning ministry from Durban. Also conducting evangelistic ministries in South Africa are Vincent Stanley near Johannesburg, Hiram Ramage at Kimberley, Ashwel Beaton near Paarl, and his older brother, Weldon Beaton, in

Individual and Family Self-Supporting Work

Port Elizabeth, and Gordon Hunt in Vredenberg.

The Spinks family, from Australia, have established a ministry in Kenya. Ralph and the other members of the family have opened an orphanage and school and are involved in many other soul-winning initiatives and educational and health training programs for the Lord. In Zambia, Betty Hewitt, an English nurse, has conducted her own ministry which also extended into Malawi. Sister Hewitt now continues this work in Kenya. David Wilson from the United States works for the Lord as a self-supporting minister in Zambia. He has now been in this part of God's mission field for many years. Trustmore Parangeta, a Hartland graduate, has an evangelistic outreach in Zimbabwe. The Elder Marc Coleman family has ministered in Thailand and West Africa. Marc is a Hartland graduate. Of course there are also the many families sponsored by Frontier Missions which have accepted the challenge to go to the areas of the world which are unentered or have few believers of our faith.

There are family ministries where parents, and children, as they grow up, commit their lives to self-supporting ministry. Examples of such ministries are the Rosenthal family in Germany. Not only do they do a fine work in Germany, which includes holding camp meetings and other meetings in Germany, as well as other parts of Europe, but they are also strongly engaged in translating present truth literature into the German language. Further, the three sons have done extensive ministry, especially in Spain and Bolivia. In Ecuador, the Orellana family has worked together in the southern part of that country, and the Salazar siblings, Esteban, David and Stephanie, all graduates of Hartland College, have raised up a training school near the capital city, Quito.

In the United States, there are many literature warriors such as Joe de Guerre in New York, and David Lee in Pennsylvania. Others, such as Cody Francis in the Western United States, have a travelling evangelistic ministry. Ray and Judy De Carlo from Maryland operate an evangelistic training program in various parts of the world. Ray is a Hartland graduate. Jessie Ravencroft, another Hartland graduate, from

Oregon, has a successful soul-winning ministry as a Bible Worker. Pastor Rogers Ballou, yet another Hartland graduate, has a church and evangelistic ministry in Sacramento, California. Dr. Larry and Gwen Hawkins conduct a strong home-school and health ministry from Washington state as does Jeanie Cook.

In Central America (Honduras), the Willis family, Joe and Elsa, former Hartland staff, are conducting a soul winning ministry established upon the health message. The McGintys have a travelling ministry in various parts of Latin America. The Robles brothers are conducting a health ministry with their families in Nicaragua. Brother Joseph and his wife have their ministry on the east coast of Nicaragua in the city of Bluefields. Sherry Trueblood, another Hartland graduate, has continued to minister on various continents of the world as a Bible worker, medical minister and Christian teacher.

The Restrepo family ministers primarily in Venezuela and Colombia. Elder Norberto Restrepo worked for many years as a denominational minister and Bible professor. He now leads a ministry in Venezuela with his wife, Nelsy, a physician, and their two married sons, David and Norberto, Jr. (Tico). Tico has now returned to their native Colombia where he and his wife, Ivonne, conduct another educational and health ministry. David ministers with his parents and his physician wife, Giovanna, in their own ministry.

The Aurilio family minister in Forteleza, Brazil. Elder Francisco Aurilio was for many years a denominational minister, but now he is operating his own self-supporting ministry with his wife and grown sons in this large northern city of Brazil. They are also operating a radio and television ministry. Also in Fortaleza, Brazil, the Herculano family has developed a publishing and translational ministry and are witnessing both to Seventh-day Adventists and those not of our faith. There certainly is an unlimited scope for individuals, husbands and wives, and families, to raise up ministries which will witness in their local community or, in some cases, other parts of the world—ministries which will do a great work in the hastening of the coming of Jesus.

Individual and Family Self-Supporting Work

Sebastian and Cynthia Teh have ministered for many years to China, and the Wong Kok Boon family is ministering in China in a language school. Both husbands are Hartland graduates. Bruce Hammer has worked for many years in a soul-seeking ministry in Taiwan. The David and Peter Joseph families have operated their ministries in India at Hyderabad and Madras respectively. Brother David conducts schools and literature ministries, and Brother Peter youth and evangelistic ministries. The Timothy Tharasingh family operate an orphanage and school in the state of Tamil Nadu. One of the daughters in that ministry, Tania, is a Hartland graduate. The Pedrin brothers David, Basil and Michael operate a literature and teaching ministry to the Seventh-day Adventist Church and to the world with their original home base of Bangalore. This is also the soul-winning ministry of the Charles Dharasingh family in Mangalore.

Malebone Laing has conducted soul-winning ministry, education and training schools for workers in many parts of the world while his sister Nellie has engaged in teaching. They hail from Sabah, East Malaysia and both are Hartland graduates.

If every Seventh-day Adventist were ignited by the challenge of a world to be warned and an invitation to be given, the gospel commission would soon be completed. Every individual and family is a potential missionary unit who, under the Holy Spirit's power, can mightily impact the world. I pray that all readers of this handbook will gain the vision of what God has called them to fulfill as part of the remnant church. There is an excuse for no one.

These are just a few examples of committed Seventh-day Adventists located on every inhabited continent who are successfully taking hold of the challenge to work for the hastening of the soon return of our blessed Savior. I pray that every reader who is not engaged in ministry will capture such a vision. This is Christ's commission to every professor of the three angel's message. The times demand decided action. The signs portend that Jesus is returning soon, very soon.

Shake off your spiritual lethargy. Work with all your

might to save your own souls and the souls of others. It is no time now to cry, "Peace and safety." It is not silver-tongued orators that are needed to give this message. The truth in all its pointed severity must be spoken. Men of action are needed—men who will labor with earnest, ceaseless energy for the purifying of the church and the warning of the world. *Testimonies*, Vol. 5, 187.

SUMMARY

1. All able-bodied, clear minded Seventh-day Adventists have a calling from God to share the gospel of the three angels to the world.
2. God can work through individuals as well as families to do a mighty work for Him.
3. The advantages of home-based ministries include,
   a. The ministry can be operated inexpensively.
   b. The ministry can be operated in the home or from the home.
   c. It provides a wide variety of ministries including Bible studies, literature distribution, health, tape, CD, video and DVD ministry, radio and television ministry, website ministry, telephone ministry, children ministry, education ministry.
4. It provides a wonderful parental training opportunity to the children in the family.
5. It also provides a bonding of the family members as they unite together in ministry.
6. Individual and family ministry is not limited to home ministry. It also can include foreign missionary work.

Chapter 8

Larger Institutional Self-Supporting Ministries

WHILE God has called for individual and family ministries, He has also called some into wider-based and more expansive ministries. Sister White strongly endorsed and supported such ministries. She sometimes called self-supporting ministries the "irregular lines" while designating denominational work as "regular lines." The use of the term *irregular* was by no means used derogatorily by Sister White. There were times when she urged that if we cannot finish the work with the "regular lines" we need to go forward with the "irregular lines."

> God is displeased with the spirit you have manifested. Your insinuations and criticisms are most unbecoming. When you ought to be a teacher, you have need that one teach you. Do you know that you are criticizing the work of a man who has been visited by the angels of the Lord? Who has sent you to a field where a good work is in progress, to show your zeal by tearing it in pieces? If this is working in the "Regular lines", it is high time that we worked in irregular lines.
>
> *Spalding and Magan Collection*, 194

> I want my brethren to begin to understand some things for themselves. God alone, by the quickening, vivifying influence of His Holy Spirit, can enable men to distinguish between the sacred and the common. God alone can make men understand that working on regular lines has led to irregular practices. God alone can make men's minds as they should be. The time has come when we should hear less in favor of the regular lines. If we can get away from the regular lines into something which, though ir-

regular, is after God's order, it may cut away something of the irregular working which has led away from Bible principles. *Manuscript Releases,* Vol. 20, 143

The first well-known self-supporting work she supported was that of her very own elder surviving son, James Edson White (1849–1928). Edson had followed a somewhat erratic course in his life. He had at times been a significant frustration to his father, James White, and was known to be at the least a poor financial manager and at the worst financially irresponsible. However, again the Lord's Spirit came upon him and he gained a deep burden for working for the "colored" (Afro-American) people in the southern part of the United States. In many ways these people were greatly neglected in the early spread of the three angels' messages and the everlasting gospel. In the 1890s, in association with Brother W. O. Palmer, he traveled down the Mississippi River and the Cumberland River, bringing the gospel from their mission boat "The Morning Star" which they had built. Sister White had greatly endorsed and encouraged her son. She also provided funds from her offerings and tithes to help support the ministry called "The Southern Missionary Society." Many precious souls were won to the Lord as a result of this ministry which continued for over a decade and a half from 1895.

> It has been presented to me for years that my tithe was to be appropriated by myself to aid the white and colored ministers who were neglected and did not receive sufficient properly to support their families. When my attention was called to aged ministers, white or black, it was my special duty to investigate into their necessities and supply their needs. . . .
>
> In regard to the colored work in the South, that field has been and is still being robbed of the means that should come to the workers in that field. If there have been cases where our sisters have appropriated their tithe to the support of the ministers working for the colored people in the South, let every man, if he is wise, hold his peace.

> I have myself appropriated my tithe to the most needy cases brought to my notice. I have been instructed to do this, and as the money is not withheld from the Lord's treasury, it is not a matter that should be commented upon.
> *Manuscript Releases*, Vol. 2, 109

Sister White was instrumental in the establishment of Madison College which was operated from 1904 by the Nashville Agricultural Normal Institute Corporation as a self-supporting institution. The idea came from a very prominent physician of that era, Dr. David Paulson, who was associated with Hinsdale Sanitarium in Illinois. The idea was taken up by Professors Edward Sutherland and Percy Magan and urged by Sister White. Property was purchased beside the town of Madison in northern Tennessee where they established this Institution which was to become known as Madison Institute. Just as Avondale College in Australia had been established as a model denominational school, so too was Madison College in Tennessee established as a pattern self-supporting school. Sister White had this to say about it,

> The work that the laborers had accomplished at Madison has done more to give a correct knowledge of what an all-round education means than any other school that has been established by Seventh-day Adventists in America. The Lord has given these teachers in the South an education that is of highest value, and it is a training that God would be pleased to have all our youth receive.
> *Manuscript Releases*, Vol. 11, 182

There was much misunderstanding and opposition from the top leadership of the General Conference. However, Sister White strongly endorsed this institution and wrote pointed letters to leaders who either did not understand, or were opposed to the work at this college.

> I do not charge any one with an intention to do wrong, but from the light I have received, I can say that there is danger that some will criticize unjustly the work of our brethren and sisters connected with the school at Madison. Let every encouragement possible be given to those

who are engaged in an effort to give children and youth an education in the knowledge of God and of His law.
The Madison School, Special Testimonies, Series B, No. 11, 17

Oftentimes in the past the work which the Lord designed should prosper has been hindered because men have tried to place a yoke upon their fellow workers who did not follow the methods which they supposed to be the best.
Ibid., 27

Let us be careful, brethren, lest we counterwork and hinder the progress of others, and so delay the sending forth of the gospel message. This has been done, and this is why I am now compelled to speak so plainly. *Ibid.,* 31

Sadly, during the course of Madison's existence, serious mistakes were made. No greater mistake was made than, under the pressure of what is now Loma Linda University, Dr. Sutherland reluctantly agreed that the institution would be accredited by the Southern Association of Schools and Colleges. This triggered a series of events which led it ultimately to close in 1964. (See Colin Standish, *The Vision and the Providences,* Hartland Publications.)

It is said that about one hundred and fifty self-supporting units, some small, some larger, were spawned from this parent institution. Madison Institute operated a college in which, if necessary, their students could work their way through school without having to pay any fees. It operated a sanitarium, a health-food factory and many and varied industries. Thus it laid the foundation for other such multi-divisional institutions. Today, in the United States and overseas, there are a number of such multi-divisional institutions. These include Wildwood Institute in Wildwood, Georgia, which operates a small training school, a hospital, a wellness center and a farm. This institution was commenced in 1941 by Elder William Frazee; Uchee Pines in Seale, Alabama, commenced by Drs. Calvin and Agatha Thrash, offers health programs and educational training programs; Weimar Institute in Weimar, California, offers college and academy education, the

Newstart Lifestyle Center. Other smaller institutions include Eden Valley in Loveland, Colorado, and various academies often associated with small industries. These include Ouachita Hills near Amity, Arkansas, Laurelbrook Academy near Dayton, Tennessee, Heritage Academy near Monterey, Tennessee, Harbert Hills Academy near Savannah, Tennessee, Oklahoma Academy near Harrah, Oklahoma, Country Haven Academy near Pasco, Washington, and Fountain View Academy in British Columbia, Canada.

There are other institutions overseas most of which are small but doing a fine work for the Lord. These include the health and orphanage institute, East African Mission, in Kenya founded by Ralph Spinks; the health institute, Aenon, located near Malaka, Malaysia, founded by David Fam; the Seventh-day Adventist Laymen Uplifting True Education (SALUTE) institute in Tamil Nadu, India, founded by Timothy Tharasingh; Riverside Farms in Zambia; Higher Ground Ministries in Sydney, Australia established by Scott Charlesworth, Mark Roberts and Lyle Southwell; Edessa International, a web-site college program established by Dr. Barry Harker in Queensland, Australia; Highwood Institute near Melbourne, Australia, a training College and health center, founded by Russell; Fundacion Las Delicias in Venezuela founded by Elder Norberto and Dr. Nelsy Restrepo; an institution by the same name established by their son Tico Restrepo and his wife Ivonne in Colombia.

Colin has had the privilege of ministering for many years at Hartland Institute which is one of the most diverse of the self-supporting institutions operating with five divisions: a college, a well-ness center, a publishing house, world missions division and stewardship ministry division.

In almost all of these institutions there is a strong agricultural emphasis. Some of them operate a diversity of industries, commercial businesses and trades. These institutions operate with small staff, some no more than four or five staff members, to scores of staff such as at Hartland Institute. Larger institutions obviously offer a much broader scope of ministry. Speaking of Hartland Institute, it has in its twenty-one-year history ministered in over one hundred countries of the world, and has educated students from almost fifty countries of the world in its college. Evangelistic and revival meetings and extension schools have been conducted on every continent and in many countries on each continent.

The larger the institution the more diversity of talents, skills and training are among its staff members and therefore the broader can be the scope of the ministry. Larger self-supporting institutions necessitate a wide range of staff backgrounds including administrative skills, financial expertise, teachers, health educators, those with publishing skills and a wide range of expertise in trades and industries. However, because of the size of the institution, the diversity of its activities and the large number of personnel needed to operate them, the organizational machinery is far more complicated and the financial needs are very critical to the viability and long-term continuation.

As the influence of an institution increases and the spread of its ministries widens, there will be increasing attention given to it by the denominational leaders. Every effort should be made to work in harmony with faithful denominational workers. All this must be accomplished while giving attention first to following divine instruction, which can never be compromised without dangerous consequences.

Whereas in a small family or individual ministry, the issue of interpersonal differences is minimized, such differences can create great tension and difficulty in a larger self-supporting ministry. Much experience is needed especially among the key administrative staff in such institutions. Even among staff with background experience it is often that few, if any, have had experience in pioneering a self-supporting ministry. Sacrifice, frugality, ingenuity, combined with faith and trust in God are key elements necessary to the success of the infant enterprise.

Satan is ever there to bring mistakes and discouragement into the equation which may lead to decisions and actions which can sow the seeds of failure. It must be remembered that in a large institution most of the missteps are exhibited in interpersonal conflict, often the result of dictatorial leadership. We have seen a number of institutions where these dangerous characteristics have been evident. It is inevitable that in these circumstances the institution becomes the length and breadth of one man, and loyalty to that man becomes an absolute requirement. Those who dissent and persistently seek to address a different agenda will inevitably be squeezed out of the institution. There is no room for dictatorship in a truly God-centered institution. We will focus in subsequent chapters upon specific principles which we believe have been most successful in the three self-supporting institutions in which we have served—Weimar Institute in California, Hartland Institute in Virginia and Remnant Herald, Melbourne, Australia.

SUMMARY

1. God uses the "irregular lines" when the "regular lines" lose their effectiveness.
2. Sister White and others supported the first self-supporting institute, Southern Missionary Society, commenced after the establishment of the denominational work with tithes and offerings.
3. Large, multi-divisional institutions require much startup capital and a stable operating income.
4. The larger the institute, the greater the difficulty to attract well-qualified, dedicated staff. But this must be a top priority.
5. Rivalry between divisions must be avoided at all cost. Division leaders are duty-bound to work together in unity.
6. The larger the institute, the greater the opportunity for interpersonal conflict. These should be resolved quickly in the fear of the Lord and according to His Word.
7. All staff must be provided a voice in the development and operation of the institution.
8. The larger and more successful an institution, the greater the likelihood of denominational misperceptions of self-

supporting work.
9. Every effort must be made to work harmoniously with denominational brethren without compromising a plain divine instruction.
10. Never must concessions be made to denominational or self-supporting leaders if they conflict with divinely inspired principles.

Chapter 9

Developing a College or an Academy

SISTER White foresaw that there would be schools of a different order established toward the end of earth's history.

> The plan of the schools we shall establish in these closing years of the message is to be of an entirely different order from those we have instituted.
> *Counsels to Parents, Teachers, and Students*, 532

It is clear that these institutions will be different from those which we have established in our past history. They will educate men and women under the divine pattern which will truly forward the work of God. They are to be established after the pattern of the Eden School and the schools of the prophets, not after the pattern of the world, nor after the pattern of our existing denominational schools. These are to be schools which faithfully follow all the principles of Scripture and Spirit of Prophecy, riveted upon the principles of Christ our Righteousness, following every divine principle of truth and righteousness. These institutions will lead to the adoption of every God-given principle of life, and will come up to every point of spiritual belief focused upon the everlasting gospel of the three angels' messages and upholding all the great pillars of our faith including the Sabbath, the state of the dead, the sanctuary message, the Second Coming, righteousness by faith and the law of God.

Such an institution must avoid at all costs the myriads of winds of doctrine which are centered upon by many who claim to be loyal to present truth. Such errors include:

1   Keeping of the pre-Calvary feast days;
2   Insistence upon using only the Hebrew names of God the Father and God the Son;
3   Using literal time rather than the day-year principle for some end-time prophecies;
4   Insistence that Christ died on Wednesday;
5   Insistence that Christ is not the eternal Son of God;
6   Denying that the Holy Spirit is the third member of the Godhead;
7   Claims that we should keep the Sabbath using Jerusalem time;
8   Questioning that the first beast of Revelation chapter 13 is the Papacy;
9   Questioning that the United States is the second beast of Revelation chapter 13.

While these institutions will be devoid of legalistic emphasis upon salvation by rules or reform, nevertheless, as the love of God will pervade the institution they will come up to every principle of reform which God has mandated. These reforms will include Sabbath reform, health reform, recreational reform, dress reform and social relations reform. No one should be chosen to lead such a school unless he or she has thoroughly read and studied the four educational books prepared by Sister White—*Education; Counsels to Parents, Teachers and Students; Fundamentals of Christian Education;* and *Counsels on Education*. Other books which would prove very helpful include E. A. Sutherland's books, *Living Fountains and Broken Cisterns;* and *Studies in Christian Education*; and the book we have written, *Adventism Imperiled*. It is futile to commence not having an educator with proven leadership skills and unwavering loyalty to the principles of God-centered education. Any institution which commences short of the paradigm is almost certain never to achieve the paradigm and therefore to drift further away from it.

Every true Christian education program will comprise three indispensable segments: First, a Christ-centered curriculum with the Bible at the hub and foundation of every subject taught; Second, a vocational and work-study segment with useful manual labor, with a special emphasis on agriculture replacing all forms of competitive sports. Staff should take time to work with the students; Third, an outreach training program where every student is trained to employ what he or she is learning in the field of Christian witness and service. All students should strive to be proven soul winners before they graduate. Any curriculum which does not contain all three of these divisions will be unbalanced and will fall short of the paradigm.

Of all the practical areas which Sister White focused upon, agriculture and gardening were paramount. Every educational program must provide for the teaching of students to grow their own gardens effectively. This includes the college level, for today many youth have been deprived of the opportunity to master this important feature of education. In all boarding institutions, strong efforts should be made to provide most of the food for the cafeteria and for the staff.

No student, having completed elementary school, should be ignorant of the main features of our faith. By the end of academy or high-school, all students should be experienced and proven workers for God and by the time they have completed college, each should have proven ability to be teachers and leaders in the things of God. True Christian educators will not be training students primarily for a profession, a career, an occupation or a job. Rather, they will be training young people to fulfill their God-given calling which He has placed upon their lives and service. No teacher can be satisfied unless all students have been led to the footstool of Jesus. This is developed first through an extensive education in the Word of God so that each student will know the saving truths of the Scripture and will believe that God, through His Son, is providing salvation for him or her.

Further, students should be led to the commitment of their lives to God, learning how to listen to His voice and follow in His steps. Fourth, every student must be trained for successful witness and service. Every teacher must evidence a compassion for the students who are struggling, and exert special efforts to encourage them along the Christian pathway. Sometimes the most difficult students, when surrendered to the Lord, make the greatest and most effective workers for God.

Wherever possible, young people should be trained extensively in a practical program with thorough education in all the essential truths of the gospel. This cannot be accomplished in a short course, although short courses may be very effective for older and more experienced church members. Contemplate these statements:

> Educated workers who are consecrated to God can do service in a greater variety of ways and can accomplish more extensive work than can those who are uneducated. Their discipline of mind places them on vantage ground.
> *Ministry of Healing*, 150

> The times demand an intelligent, educated ministry, not novices, . . . The world is becoming educated to a high standard of literary attainment. . . . This state of things calls for the use of every power of the intellect; for it is keen minds, under the control of Satan, that the minister will have to meet.
> *Testimonies*, Vol. 5, 528

> It is not in harmony with God's purpose that all should plan to spend exactly the same length of time, whether three, four, or five years, in preparation, before beginning to engage in active field work. Some, after studying for a time, can develop more rapidly by working along practical lines in different places, under the supervision of experienced leaders, than they could by remaining in an institution.
> *Counsels to Parents, Teachers, and Students*, 469

Many more schools "of a different order" will be established around the world to fulfill the prophecy that such schools will be raised up by God at the end of time to train the youth who, under the indwelling power of the latter rain, will spread the gospel invitation to the whole world.

Developing a College or an Academy

SUMMARY

1. Schools, different from our past schools, will be established before the close of probation.
2. These schools will follow the divine pattern set out in the Bible and Spirit of Prophecy.
3. Only present-truth-believing and -practicing administrators and staff will form the faculty of such schools.
4. The primary focus will be the conversion of every student and the preparation of each student for effective soul-winning service.
5. Staff will eschew winds of doctrine.
6. Staff will train the students in an understanding of the true reforms including Sabbath, health, dress, recreational and social relations reform.
7. All staff must study the divine counsels for education contained in *Education, Counsels to Parents and Teachers, Fundamentals of Christian Education* and *Counsels on Education*.
8. The schools will provide three elements.
   a. An in-depth Bible-centered academic curriculum.
   b. A strong vocational training component including agriculture.
   c. A practical soul-winning training program.
9. The chief goals of these schools will be—
   a. To provide a strong knowledge and understanding of God and His Word.
   b. To lead every pupil to the footstool of Christ.
   c. To educate each student in service for God and man.

Chapter 10
Establishing a Health Center

AS with college leadership, a well qualified staff is crucial in a health center. The same dedication and soul-winning motivation must be inherent in all who are chosen for leadership and staff positions in a health center. This is even more important than the quality of the facility and equipment, although, of course, adequate working equipment must be available. Where accurate calibration is required, regular checks of accuracy must be made. Many successful health centers have been faithfully commenced in an adequately sized home where a number of bedrooms are available for health guests.

The counsel of the Lord is that such health centers should be located in the country. The rural environment is conducive to restoration of body and soul.

> The great medical institutions in our cities, called sanitariums do but a small part of the good they might do were they located where the patients could have the advantages of outdoor life. I have been instructed that sanitariums are to be established in many places in the country, and that the work of these institutions will greatly advance the cause of health and righteousness.
>
> *Counsels on Health*, 169

Our sanitariums also should be located in the country, and the grounds around the buildings should be beautified by ornamental trees which will invite the patients to sit in their shade. It is impossible to overrate the influence for

good that these advantages exert.
Sermons and Talks, Vol. 2, 225

A health center can be established in a previously occupied facility if sufficient funds are available for purchase and alterations. A new facility does not have to be elaborately decorated or extravagantly furnished.

> Wealth or high position, costly equipment, architecture or furnishings, are not essential to the advancement of the work of God; neither are achievements that win applause from men and administer to vanity. Worldly display, however imposing, is of no value in God's sight.
> *Ministry of Healing*, 36, 37

> The sanitarium needs not his [Dr. Caro's] extravagant ideas. Everything about the institution is to be neat and tasteful, but no extravagance is to be shown in the furnishings. *Manuscript Release*, Vol. 7, 61

However, health centers should be pleasant and representative, well maintained and cared for. Each room should have a view of the rural surroundings. Such views are therapeutic.

Remember that a health facility is not a medical facility *per se*. The emphasis of these centers is upon preventive measures and restorative healing. The focus should be upon the eight natural remedies—pure water, fresh air, adequate rest, temperance, moderate exposure to sunlight, physical exercise, healthy nutrition and dependence upon divine power. At Hartland we were privileged to be able to have our institute name as an acronym for the eight natural remedies—

- H   hydrotherapy
- A   fresh air
- R   rest
- T   temperance
- L   light (sun)
- A   activity
- N   nutrition
- D   dependence upon divine power.

If the institute is solely a health center, it may be possible to choose a name which is also an acronym for the eight natural remedies.

The Remnant Herald has developed an acronym for the eight natural remedies which uses only single words. It is:

M moderation
Y yield
A air
N nutrition
S sunlight
W water
E exercise
R rest

The "yield," of course, is the yielding to divine guidance and power.

The health facility should have an experienced leader not only with a commitment for God's special remedies, but he or she must also possess an experienced and successful business background. A great plus is marketing ability. As with any organization, much of the length and breadth of success depends upon quality marketing linked with faith and prayer in and for God's guiding power. The ministry is not limited to the Seventh-day Adventist community. It must reach out to the community at large. Especially should it focus upon those who are employed in high-stress responsibilities. A Christian health program will be invaluable not only to the physical needs of those it serves, but also their emotional and spiritual needs.

Seek free advertising for the health center. Send news releases to newspapers, health journals, radio and television outlets. Make staff personnel available for media interviews. Invite the media to your health center. Announce to health media outlets the existence of your health center, asking them to list details of your facility. Provide to them photographs of the health center, its equipment and guests. Develop an attractive website. Produce an attractive and informative brochure.

Offer your health team, making the members available

to churches of all denominations, to service clubs and community centers. These services provide effective advertising for your health center. Prepare a publication which tells the stories and testimonies of those who have been restored at your institution. Keep detailed records of physical improvement and present these in such a publication. There are a thousand and one ways which the creative mind will find to attract health guests to the institution.

All staff should be required to read all the major health and temperance books written by Sister White—*Ministry of Healing, Counsels on Health, Counsels on Diet and Foods, Medical Ministry* and *Temperance.* The studying of these books will equip them for their high and holy calling.

The staff also must be well-trained. It is essential to have skilled nutritionists and/or dieticians, hydrotherapists, massage therapists and exercise physiologists on the staff. It is advantageous to have at least one physician, preferably two. Having both a male and a female physician meets the guidelines of male physicians treating men and female physicians treating ladies. Male and female hydrotherapists and massage therapists are necessary for male and female health guests. It is possible to operate an effective wellness center without a physician, but under such circumstances even greater care must be taken in the choice of health guests. It is certainly unwise to admit the critically ill under these circumstances. They need the care of a trained medical staff. Without qualified doctors and nurses no effort should be made to carry out medical procedures. Remember always, precious lives are at stake.

In any health center, it is expedient to be careful to refrain from making exaggerated claims concerning the likely outcome of the treatment. In the present climate in the Western World, for example, any advertising of cancer cures can lead to very serious prosecutions as the great majority of these claims are bogus. Some preventive health workers have actually been jailed for such claims. This is especially likely to happen if the health guest dies, even though he or she might well have died when under hospital care. Claims of cure made either in writing or verbally can lead to negative repercussions. Let the results speak for themselves. Let those health guests proclaim what the program has accomplished for them. Let them write their testimony. If they have the testimony of their personal physician let that be spread far and wide. What a wellness center can do is to make justifiable and accurate claims that the treatment seeks to improve the immune system so that the body itself is in the position to fight disease more effectively. Almost all health centers which we know have had some limited success with cancer patients, especially those guests who have come in the early stage of their disease.

We do know that there are certain herbs which are helpful to particular physical conditions and they should be used in the appropriate cases. Remember that herbs are effective only if they possess some curative agent. Often, marketed herbs are not produced under strict quality control and are not always scientifically tested for their medicinal value.

However carefully chosen the claims you make, the main basis of therapy in a wellness center should be within the parameters of the eight natural remedies. Any form of therapy for which the therapist is not adequately trained should be avoided. There are many areas where serious hurt can be done by novices. We have heard of a number of these cases at various institutions where inexperienced or careless staff have put the health guest at risk. A simple mistake such as applying heat to a fevered patient rather than ice packs to bring down the temperature, is one example. Another risk involves the testing of blood sugar levels where the testing machine has not been properly calibrated, thus giving a false reading. If the blood sugar level is recorded as high when it is low, the giving of increased doses of insulin can be fatal.

With patients suffering hypertension (high blood pressure) care especially must be taken with those who are at risk for serious cardiac problems. Hydrotherapy, for example, will need to be moderated with such health guests. The use of fever treatments can be very dangerous in some circumstances and certainly is not a "cure-all." The patient must be constantly monitored in such treatments. An inexperienced person in training, undertaking any procedure, must be carefully monitored by an experienced and well qualified staff member.

We have seen wonderful recoveries and regeneration of those who have been led to a change of life-style. By far the most effective results come from those who are suffering from lifestyle diseases such as hypertension, obesity, high cholesterol and/or triglycerides, diabetes and cardiac problems. Evidence is increasing that life-style change can reverse many diseases. Over a period of time, the effects of occluded blood vessels can be reversed by major changes in life-style.

These programs, so simple in their design, also are a great help to those seeking weight loss. Health guests have been restored who suffered from autoimmune diseases which rarely are effectively treated by conventional medications. One woman, with a large ulcer on her thigh which had failed to respond to the best efforts of physicians at a large university hospital was fully restored and healed in a couple of months by the simple treatment at Hartland Wellness Center. One of our physicians was invited to explain the treatment which had been so successful, to the doctors at the university medical center which had previously ineffectively treated the patient.

The program is wonderfully beneficial for those who do not exhibit any specific disease symptoms. Some health guests come to wellness centers to establish a more productive lifestyle which will safeguard them for the future and will safeguard the quality of their life as they age. It is not always easy to convince apparently healthy people to take part in such programs. But the old adage "An ounce of prevention is worth a pound of cure" is certainly appropriate in the area of health. This is the reason why at Hartland Wellness Center we offer regular training sessions for teenagers and those in their early twenties. The earlier an adequate and optimal lifestyle is chosen, the more benefits will accrue to the reformed subjects.

Every program should provide much more than the theory. There must be hands-on experience and training sessions for all those involved in the program. This is especially true in the dietary area. It is our duty to teach the virtues and blessings of a vegan diet. It is an altogether higher level of instruction to show how to prepare vegan food which is attractive, tasty and satisfying. Therefore much time should be spent in training health guests, many of whom have been flesh eaters all their lives, how to make such a dramatic change in their diet. It is understandable that such a major life-style change is challenging. Old habits are hard to eliminate. Therefore every effort must be made to teach the preparation not only of healthy food, but also of appetizing food.

Every health program must have a follow-up regime where the health guests are contacted after they have left. There is always a rate of attrition as some health guests regress step by step to their own old failed habits. This regression can be significantly reduced by encouraging telephone contacts from the wellness center or by pairing the health guests and asking them, at least on a weekly basis, to contact each other for mutual encouragement. Of course, above all, health guests should be encouraged to pray daily for power from God in order to maintain divinely established health habits. It is also helpful for some to return to the health center for short refresher courses as often as once each year.

It is most important that regular checks are made of the health guests during their stay at the wellness center. When new guests arrive a panel of blood tests should be taken together with other indices such as lung capacity, exercise tolerance, the step test, taking into account initial pulse rate, end-of-test pulse rate and time to recovery to the resting pulse rate. Checks should be made daily of blood pressure and blood sugar levels (for diabetics). Cholesterol and triglyceride levels should be recorded at the beginning and end of the program. Other needed profiles should be carefully monitored according to specific conditions. It is wise to ask health guests to bring with them, or preferably send before their admission, their latest medical reports. This helps the staff to plan for the specific needs of the incoming guests.

There is a further dimension that must not be neglected in the ministry to health guests—that is the area of emotional help. The best Christian principles of emotional health must be addressed from the perspective that God is interested in all facets of our life—physical, social, emotional, intellectual and spiritual. The Bible therefore contains all the best principles to meet the needs of all our lives. These principles should be shared with the guests. We have written a book which will be a great help to you in helping those suffering from depression, guilt and many other forms of emotional illness. It is entitled, *God's Solution for Depression, Guilt and Mental Illness*.

One of the most exciting moments of a program arrives toward the end of the session when a new battery of blood and other tests are measured. Almost inevitably there are great improvements in the health guests' blood profiles and this in itself is a wonderful motivation for them to continue in their lifestyle reforms after they have returned to their homes.

We must not forget the importance of the health guests' spiritual life. Often the health guests are not only broken in body but also in spirit, and are emotionally and often morally debilitated. The servant of the Lord has counseled that the spiritual ministry should not first be directed to the distinctive doctrines which we hold, but rather upon leading hearts to Christ and faith in His power.

> When the Spirit of God works on the mind of the afflicted one, and he inquires for truth, let the physician work for the precious soul as Christ would work for it. Do not urge upon him any special doctrine, but point him to Jesus as a sin-pardoning Saviour. Angels of God will make impressions on the human mind. *Medical Ministry*, 188–189

Some health programs have watered down or almost eliminated the spiritual part of the program. That is not so at Hartland; indeed our philosophy is just the opposite. It is true that we have had Jews, Moslems, atheists and agnostics and many Christians not of our faith in our programs. Yet we have found that, for the most part, the health guests are very much blessed by the spiritual services morning and evening. No health guest is required to attend these worships against his or her desire. However, we have found that a majority come to these worships and there have been those who have told us that though they are grateful for the excellent physical improvement which they have made, they realize that even more important has been revitalization of their spiritual life. We invite health guests to come to church with us on Sabbath and not a few, not of our faith, accept the invitation. There will be those who will ask questions concerning the Seventh-day Adventist beliefs and when they do we should do everything we can to answer those questions.

We have also seen numbers of Seventh-day Adventists who have become cold and listless in their spiritual lives who have been spiritually revitalized as a result of the program. A number of our health guests have accepted the Seventh-day Adventist faith and become baptized members. Personally Colin has had the opportunity of participate in such baptisms.

Programs should be established whenever possible for the training of others in health ministry. Such a course will multiply the work which we know will be the final avenue by which the gospel will penetrate to the ends of the earth. Even today it is a real opportunity for spiritual blessing and conversions.

SUMMARY

1 Choice of staff for a health center is even more important than facility or equipment.
2 Choose a country location.
3 A health center can be established in
   a. A commodious home.
   b. An existing building which has been remodeled for the purpose, or
   c. A new building pleasant and representative, but it does not need to be elaborate nor expensive.
4 The emphasis is upon preventive and restorative health

methods using primarily the eight natural remedies.
5. Herbal treatment is helpful in certain conditions.
6. Seek to advertise widely. Use free advertising as much as possible.
   a. News releases to newspapers, health journals, radio and television are often free.
   b. Make staff available for interviews.
   c. Provide information with suitable photographs for distribution.
   d. Prepare an attractive web page.
   e. Prepare a well designed brochure and information packet.
   f. Make the health team available to churches, community organizations and service clubs.
   g. Prepare a book with personal stories from the center.
7. All staff should be required to read inspired health and temperance books including *Ministry of Healing, Counsels on Diet and Foods, Medical Ministry, Counsels on Health* and *Temperance*.
8. If operating a health center without a certified physician, care must be exercised not to accept the critically ill and not to undertake major medical procedures.
9. Be conservative in the claims made. Emphasize the building up of the immune system and the lowering of blood sugar, blood pressure, cholesterol, triglycerides and weight and the increasing of physical strength and other such measurable improvements.
10. Carefully record and keep statistics of the improvements in every patient and the collective averages of improvements.
11. All health programs should provide practical training in simple treatments and vegan food preparation.
12. All programs should provide post-treatment follow-up inquiries and encouragement. Partners can help each other and telephone contact from the health center staff is most helpful.
13. Seek to help both the spiritual and emotional needs of

the health guests. This effort will supplement physical progress.
14 Seek to train youth and others as medical missionaries.

Chapter 11

Establishing a Publishing and/or a Printing House

LIKE the medical missionary work, the printed page will play a leading role in the finishing of the gospel commission. Some may believe that with the rapid escalation of the use of electronic means of communication, the printed page will decrease significantly in impact. While there may be a good rationale for this conclusion, nevertheless it will not negate the importance of the printed page. The Internet, e-mail, faxes, audio- and video-tapes, CDs, DVDs, radio and television certainly will play their roles in the finishing of the gospel commission. Yet there is no indication, either in the Spirit of Prophecy or in contemporary thinking, that there will be no need for the printed word. As it is today, it is not likely that the electronic media will completely overshadow the importance of the published page. The invention of the printing press was key to the development of the Reformation and the drive to bring education to the masses so that, as Tyndale put it, "Even the plowboy" could study the Word of God for himself.

While the printed page has now been used for the most abominable Satanic perversions, it is up to Christians to employ it for the proclamation of the gospel and the completion of the spread of the Word to the world. However, both the establishment of a publishing house and a printing establishment can be very costly. Hartland is not presently operating a printing press, although we have done so on a limited scale in the past. Some have done a fine work, however, with small presses such as an A. B. Dick.

Pastor George Burnside, the powerful New Zealand

evangelist, in his retirement years in Australia, made excellent use of his basement press to publish well over one hundred tracts, booklets and books which he had authored. These have been circulated widely around the world and have proven of great help in encouraging men and women to stay true to the great message of salvation which God has entrusted to our church. However, to go into major printing, which includes major book production, is another level of operation altogether. One who has successfully achieved this level is Dwight Hall, the founder and director of Remnant Publications in Michigan. This success has permitted him to do an outstanding work in publishing truth-filled literature including Spirit of Prophecy books. Not only are these sold to Seventh-day Adventist outlets but they are carried in many of the non-Seventh-day Adventist outlets. In the Czech Republic one brother has accomplished a great work in publishing and printing Spirit of Prophecy books and other truth-filled publications. However a large operation such as this does require significant up-front capital and should not be contemplated unless there is a strong likelihood of raising such capital. At Hartland we have chosen not to undertake the establishment of a printing division. There are a number of reasons for this decision that anyone contemplating such an undertaking should consider.

1 Remnant Publications is a fine printing and publishing house where most of the books we publish have been printed.
2 To find well qualified and experienced printers has proven to be very difficult. There are few enough to go around in the Seventh-day Adventist denomination and to put out a large expense for printing equipment and buildings with the knowledge of the scarcity of printers willing to sacrifice to get the truth out, could lead to frustrating results, for if there were a sudden departure from the team it might be difficult, or nearly impossible, to find a suitable replacement.
3 We have watched the sincere efforts of other fine institutions which have expended considerable amounts of scarce

funds for printing equipment only in the end to have to close them down. Now, if the one to start an operation is very familiar with printing and has a knowledgeable staff, we certainly would not think to discourage such a one. But for inexperienced people it may prove a major disappointment and be associated with great loss of resources should the printing project fail. There is a great need for dedicated young people to be trained in the printing trade.

To run a publishing house is a major undertaking. Once again the leader and staff must first and foremost be faithful and devoted Seventh-day Adventists. They must possess an excellent knowledge of the messages of salvation because they will have to make important judgments concerning that which will be suitable for publication.

The leader needs strong, proven financial management skills as well as personnel management skills. In many ways, the publishing division has been the most difficult division at Hartland Institute to achieve these goals. However, it is very stable at this time. If a ministry seeks to do all the pre-press desk-top publishing, it needs the services of individuals with quality skills in these areas. If, as we have, the decision is taken to operate not only the publishing house but a wholesale and retail sales operation also, financial aspects become complex. Quality inventory control must be maintained. Effective marketing is critical. Fiscal integrity is of the highest priority.

Over quite a number of years Hartland's best pre-press work has been very well accomplished by Charley Tompkins who resides in northern California. Excellent copy editors, proofreaders and cover designers are all key members of the team. At the time of writing, most of this work is undertaken off-campus although there have been times when we have had experts in-house to accomplish this work. Every publication is to represent the Lord and should be undertaken with the utmost care and efficiency. We are dealing with precious truth and all that we do must represent the quality that the Lord would expect from us.

The keeping of effective and up-to-date mailing lists, are

all important to maintain customer credibility. Special care must be exercised in choosing those who are entrusted with customer service and warehouse personnel. It is much easier to lose a dissatisfied customer than to gain a new one. Every detail is important in the area of management. Customer service staff must recognize that orders must be met promptly and be accurately supplied. When requested material is out of stock, the customer must be informed as to the date it will likely be supplied or informed that it cannot be supplied. The provision of up-to-date catalogs is mandatory to the success of the sales department. They should be attractive and briefly indicate the matters included in the books.

Hartland Institute has also commenced three periodicals, only one of which is still prepared at the Institute. The other two continue to do the work of God in other locations. The first periodical which we established was *Sabbath School Lesson Comments by Ellen White*. This was established in 1984 when Dr. Ted Wade asked if we would publish such a quarterly periodical. He had offered it to the Review and Herald Publishing Association and the Pacific Press, both of which decided against publishing it. Each day of each quarter special Spirit of Prophecy statements are provided to supplement the day's lesson. This quarterly book found a ready market because a policy decision was taken by the General Conference Sabbath School Department to greatly reduce the use of Spirit of Prophecy quotations. Subsequently, seeing the success of this publication, the Pacific Press now publishes a quarterly, *E. G. White Notes for the Sabbath School Lessons.* A significant number of subscribers still prefer our selection of quotations in *Sabbath School Lesson Comments by Ellen White*. This quarterly is now being published by Charles and Delpha Tompkins in California and they are doing an excellent work.

The second periodical was commenced as a student project called *Your Choice.* It was directed to a youthful readership. However, very quickly we realized that Hartland students did not have the time to carry out all the editorial responsibilities. For many years now this periodical has been a department of Hartland Institute under the name *Last Generation* magazine. This has become the missionary magazine of choice for many Seventh-day Adventists around the world. This is a magazine which was established upon the principles which Sister White had enunciated in the nineteenth century for the *Signs of the Times*. It is a magazine which focuses upon events transpiring in the world and evaluates them in the light of Biblical prophecy and the soon return of our Lord and Savior. It directs the reader to the necessary preparation to be ready to meet the Lord. Many subscribers have judged *Last Generation* to be the finest Seventh-day Adventist outreach periodical in the English language. The present editor is Sister Betsy Mayer.

The third publication established was the *Young Disciple* magazine, a magazine for young people approximately between the ages of ten and sixteen. This magazine is still edited by the foundational editor and conceiver of the magazine, Janet Evert. However, she, with her family, are now publishing this weekly publication at their present location in northeastern Washington state. In our evaluation it is the finest youth magazine in the English language. Many young people have been encouraged by the *Young Disciple* magazine to surrender their lives to Christ and to His communion. At the time of publishing this handbook there is an urgent need to produce magazines for younger children of the same quality of materials as is found in *Young Disciple* Magazine. Any subscription periodical requires a meticulously kept database and requires the provision of punctual renewal notices and well-kept accounts.

There are increasing numbers of young people trained at Hartland in the Christian Publication Management major. Many more will be trained in the future. These young people have a strong background in the Bible-based truths of the Seventh-day Adventist faith to support their developed skills in the publishing work. Some have emphasized the editorial side in their life's work while others have chosen to devote their talents to the technical side of publications.

SUMMARY

1. The printed page will play a major role in the finishing of the gospel proclamation.
2. Large publishing houses are costly to equip and difficult to staff and should be undertaken only by those who have strong financial and personnel resources.
3. It is possible and practical to do a great work for the Lord with small presses which can be purchased inexpensively second-hand.
4. As in any enterprise, the keeping of careful accounting is essential.
5. With on-line capabilities, aspects of publishing can effectively be carried out away from the center of the publishing house, even overseas.
6. Advertising is key to sales.
7. Keep in mind the variety of publications which may be considered.
    a. Books and booklets.
    b. Magazines and periodicals.
    c. Tracts.
    d. Tabloids.

Chapter 12
Establishing a Media Ministry

IN defining the area of focus, we will be discussing a range of ministry tools, including audio and video tapes, CDs, DVDs, the web-sites, radio and television programming and the operation of a radio or television station. An effective and inexpensive media ministry can be achieved by operating a tape ministry. This mission has been done very effectively over the years. Perhaps the best known current tape ministries are American Cassette Ministry, and Keep the Faith Ministry which was for many years operated by its founder, Elder Lawrence Nelson until 2004 when Hal Mayer became its Director and Speaker. This monthly tape ministry reaches people in many parts of the world. Seventeen to twenty thousand tapes are presently distributed monthly. All that is needed for such a ministry is good recording equipment and quality duplication material. Of course, a tape ministry, if it becomes extensive, generates a large volume of work, which includes keeping up with mailing lists, packaging, addressing, posting and receipting of donations. It can develop rapidly into more than a one-person operation.

It is important to recognize that people are now turning to CDs rather than tapes. Almost all recently manufactured cars, for example, have CD players rather than tape players installed. Keep in mind that many people listen to gospel messages while traveling in their cars. For someone seeking to start such a ministry it would be wise to consider, rather than a tape ministry, a CD ministry. CD copies can be made inexpensively, too. CDs will also have the advantage of reaching younger people who are more likely to own CD players than audio machines. Keep in mind that there is little good Christian material available for children and youth, and someone may take up the burden of preparing materials for children and youth ministries.

God's people also have increasing difficulty in finding quality sacred music. This field is wide open. However, one of the great limitations is the copyright law. It is essential to avoid any infringement of such laws. Just as audio cassettes obsoleted reel-to-reel audio players, so CDs are certain to replace audio cassettes. A similar transformation is taking place in the video industry. Video cassettes replaced films and now with the introduction of DVDs, over a period of time, they will reduce and finally eliminate the use of video tapes. In the future, new technology is bound to bring forth more advanced innovations in the fields of audio and video recording Those contemplating such ministries need to keep in mind these future trends. This is not to assume that the production of audio and video tapes should be discarded. However, those commencing such ministries will exercise vigilance to keep up with, and even be in the vanguard of these changes. For the present time, audio and video tapes, CDs and DVDs can be produced as witnessing tools.

We have a friend in Australia, Ross Corney, who for years has conducted an "on the road" ministry. He has been successful in distributing large quantities of Christian literature to men and women while supporting himself from the tapes of his music, he being an excellent soloist presenting true gospel hymns. He sings in shopping centers, malls and other places where large crowds of people are found. At the end of 2002, he informed Colin that there had been a rapid change in his sales from cassette tapes to CDs. He estimated that as high as ninety-five percent of his sales were now CDs. Hartland Institute has an active audio and video tape ministry as well as a CD and DVD ministry.

Those desirous of moving into a radio or television ministry, should undertake that outreach at whatever level their finances and support will permit. Obviously, it is possible to begin at the level of one program per week on a single local station. If this proves successful and it begins to be well supported by the listeners, then other opportunities will arise to expand this ministry. Such a program has been operating for some time, very successfully, by Elder Clark Floyd and Brother Lee Forbes in the Asheville area of North Carolina. That ministry is expanding. It began initially with a Sunday morning program on one station.

Many areas operate community based broadcast stations. Frequently, these community stations have difficulty in finding persons to operate some of their sessions. Such opportunities often arise initially at unpopular times—late at night or early in the morning. But they have the advantage of being cost free. They often open up opportunities later to take over more popular time slots.

A similar approach may be taken with television programming. It may be that such a program can commence on a small local television station and then it, too, as it is supported, has the potential to expand. We recognize that media programs including Voice of Prophecy, Faith for Today, Quiet Hour, Amazing Facts, It Is Written, and Breath of Life, all commenced as small operations, but those ministries have expanded greatly over the decades. Such ministries have the advantage of not having to run a costly radio or television station. However, the ministry usually expands when it develops its funding, to an increasing number of stations. Do not forget the advantage of using stations with satellite uplinks.

Some may be inspired to own and operate a radio station or television channel. Small radio stations can be operated fairly inexpensively. However, God may call some to commence a radio station or television channel which will present the truth in all its fullness and there may be those who have both the background and resources so to do. For example, most readers will be familiar with 3ABN which has had a very successful operation for many years now. Less well known, at least in the United States, is the radio station operated by American Ron Meyers in southeastern France close to the Swiss city of Geneva.

From time to time, the Federal Communications Commission opens up new opportunities in the United States in various regions for the operation of new radio stations. Contact with the Federal Communications Commission would determine the likelihood of times when such opportunities would be available for bid. No doubt opportunities also become available for television stations. Whichever direction is indicated, it is important to check out all the factors. These would largely determine cost. It is possible to operate localized ten-watt stations in certain places. This might prove to be productive in witness. Remember that mountainous areas can greatly reduce the listening or viewing area or would require major relay disks which would add considerably to cost. Remember also to employ staff only who give evidence of being dedicated Christians and are able to discern what is soul-winning in content. Resist any compromise in the materials presented.

In the city of Fortaleza, in northeastern Brazil, a wonderful opportunity presented itself to Pastor Francisco Aurilo Rodriguez Gomez, a self-supporting minister. He and his family were already operating a radio station sixteen hours a day. The government opened up four new cable television channels. Three were earmarked, one for the university and one each for the state senate and congress (the lower house). The fourth channel was reserved for the public for community service purposes. Pastor Aurilo submitted an application to be awarded this community channel. To his great surprise his prayers were answered and he was awarded the television station. For some reason, maybe due to lack of knowledge, in this strongly Roman Catholic city of almost three million people, his was the only application. He had wisely chosen a direction and programming which was well received. Besides religious programming he indicated that he would be offering educational, health, family life, youth and children's programs. Of course, all these fitted into the goals which he had for spreading the various facets of the Seventh-day Adventist message. The license cost him nothing. Of course he had to obtain the necessary equipment for operating that station on the cable network, a very rapidly growing network in that city and its state. It was the privilege of Remnant Herald and Hartland Institute to equally share the cost for the purchasing of this equipment. In 2002, it was our joy to witness the television station up and running. Maybe God will open up such opportunities elsewhere in the world.

Finally, we turn to the worldwide web with its enormous witnessing potential. The worldwide web has opened potentialities never dreamed of just a few decades ago. While the web is being used for unspeakable wickedness, it also offers unprecedented opportunities for Christian witness. The web, at a very minimal outlay, is available to web users all over the world. Already more than two hundred million English reading web users are potential readers of that which is placed upon the web and this number is expanding every day. The web offers a special opportunity to contact the youth for, at this point of time, younger people are more likely than older people to access the web. This should be kept in mind in presenting material on the web. Special approaches to children, including children's Bible studies and inspirational stories, would be beneficial. Also, issues important to young married couples and families offer strong opportunities. However, special approaches in no wise limit the web to just the younger generation. Yet it is important to realize the tremendous potential especially for this group.

Hartland has placed the *Great Controversy* in thirteen different languages on the web site. This includes the five languages most accessed on the web. There are many opportunities to put not only Spirit of Prophecy books on the web, but other important books which will lead people to the Seventh-day Adventist message and the end-time preparation for the kingdom of heaven. Do not forget to share the opening wedge—the health message—on the web.

One area to which we are very sensitive is the use of the web to debate Seventh-day Adventist issues which show the tragic split in thinking and practice in the Seventh-day Adventist Church. We realize that there are many efforts to defame the Seventh-day Adventist faith from those not of our faith, by former Seventh-day Adventists who are extraordinarily active in their efforts, and, sadly, by many who claim to be faithful Seventh-day Adventists but are presenting all forms of new theology and winds of doctrine. We seriously caution our people, asking that they consider the unprofitability of dialoguing back and forth on these issues. Certainly we would warn against using the web as a way to expose the tragic evidence of wickedness, worldliness and apostasy in our beloved Seventh-day Adventist Church. To do so is directly against the counsel of the servant of the Lord—that we are not to expose our "dirty linen" before others for this may in itself lead some never again to look favorably upon the Seventh-day Adventist message.

> Christians should not appeal to civil tribunals to settle differences that may arise among church members. Such differences should be settled among themselves, or by the church, in harmony with Christ's instruction. Even though injustice may have been done, the follower of the meek and lowly Jesus will suffer himself "to be defrauded" rather

than open before the world the sins of his brethren in the church.
Acts of the Apostles, 305

Publish it not to the enemies of our faith. They have no right to the knowledge of church matters, lest the weakness and errors of Christ's followers be exposed.
Testimonies, vol. 2, 57

We believe our concentration should largely focus upon presenting the pure everlasting gospel of the three angels. Such themes as the Second Coming, the state of the dead, the Sabbath, the sanctuary message and the message of Christ our Righteousness are well suited to the employment of the web. However teach each of these themes within the centrality of Christ to our salvation. We believe all faithful Seventh-day Adventists who have access to the web should be seeking to begin such a ministry. The beauty of this form of witness is that it leads to progress only as fast as the user has time to use it. It matters not that many others may be presenting the same subjects. All will present these truths in a little different manner and will no doubt be accessed by different individuals.

Even if your web site is small it can be enlarged. The ministry may be increased in its impact by linkage to other web-sites where more extensive or more in-depth studies and presentations can be found. The very volume of material will eventually arrest the attention and set some to wonder why there is so much material about the Seventh-day Adventist faith. This ministry also has the opportunity of offering Bible studies, literature, books, magazines, tracts, and periodicals either for sale or free. Try it. Those who do will discover this to be a very rewarding and effective method of ministering. And who knows that this may through witness for the Lord lead to souls whom you will present to Christ when He returns.

Another great potential is the streaming of CDs, videos and DVDs on the worldwide web. Remember that only digital material can be used. Using satelite technology, wonderful material can be streamed to all parts of the world. If it is possible to access foreign language materials this will greatly enhance your ministry. To maximize receivers and listeners, broad band technology will greatly increase the audience. A quality T1-line will be necessary. It further provides opportunity to offer products for distribution or sale including books, periodicals and other media materials. Do not forget to diversify the areas of material presented.

SUMMARY

1. Low cost media ministry.
   a. Audio, video, CD and DVD ministry. Keep in mind the demand is shifting rapidly from audio and video tapes to CDs and DVDs.
   b. Beside sermons, offer seminars, youth and children ministries programs and sacred music (be careful of copyright laws).
   c. As the ministry grows it can be too much for one person.
   d. A radio or television ministry can be conducted as little as once a week on one station and expand to others as funds become available. Remember to be ready to respond to inquiries.
   e. Using the internet to present Bible-based messages can be undertaken inexpensively. Special articles, magazines or books can also be presented to the web users.
   f. Do not use the web to expose the problems in the Seventh-day Adventist Church.
   g. Streaming CD and DVD material by satelite on the website offers major opportunities to witness all over the world.
2. High cost media ministries:
   a. Operating a radio station or network of stations.
   b. Operating a television station or network of stations.
   c. Choose converted managers and staff.
   d. Make sure all the programming is relevant to the spiritual life of listeners.
   e. Diversify programming: preaching, teaching, dia-

    logues, interviews, discussions, sacred music.
 f. Deal with current events, prophecy, Biblical truth, Christian life style, health, family life, Christian witness, youth and children's programs.

Chapter 13

Agriculture, the ABC of Ministry

WHETHER your ministry is individual, family or institutional, single-focused or multi-divisional, agriculture should play an essential role. The time will come when the "no buying and no selling" decree will be legislated. Therefore it is obligatory that all faithful Christian workers will be prepared for that eventuality. Gardening provides not only the opportunity to grow healthy food, but also provides wonderful spiritual lessons and exercise in the fresh air.

Millennia after millennia agrarian pursuits dominated the occupational and recreational activities of mankind. Survival was centered upon them; and man's dependence upon, and often struggle with, nature constituted the central issue of life. Cities were small and widely dispersed, so that the majority of the world's inhabitants lived in rural and semi-rural locations. Nature, for the most part, was not seriously disturbed, and the ecological balance was naturally maintained.

Hardly could the early geniuses of the Industrial Revolution have been expected to foresee the tidal-wave effect of their rather crude mechanical inventions. Surely none could have predicted the socio-psychological impact of these exciting discoveries, nor the effect upon life's struggles, physical development, and health.

By the early part of the twentieth century, these changes had begun to have a marked impact upon the distribution of mankind. Large industrially-based cities attracted, like a magnet, the increasing number of ruralists who were forced by economics and advancing technology to leave the soil which had been their heritage for unnumbered generations. All too often the complex psychological and sociological impact of such rapid changes was either not perceived or could not be adequately handled by government or social agencies. In fact, very few of the latter existed; and when, after World War II, social agencies proliferated, it was far too late to address a problem which now was totally confounded with the other urban issues.

There is no way that the impact of industrialization upon human experience can be adequately evaluated; but recent successful experiments with agriculture as a therapy for the mentally and physically handicapped are indices of the probable contribution of agriculture to harmonious human growth and development. While one may question Thomas Jefferson's claim that agriculture is the most democratic occupation, it is increasingly difficult to ignore the mounting evidence that the pursuits of the soil are basic to human experience.

God has provided a systematic philosophy of agriculture in education. It is surprising that a pursuit so integral to human history has been largely ignored, or perhaps taken for granted even by God's church. Ellen White has given some of the strongest reasons for agriculture in the curriculum.

> Study in agricultural lines should be the A, B, and C of the education given in our schools. This is the very first work that should be entered upon. Our schools should not depend upon imported produce, for grain and vegetables, and the fruits so essential to health.
> *Testimonies*, Vol. 6, 179

She elaborated upon this statement by stressing the value of agricultural pursuits in every major segment of life. She declared that agriculture develops practical wisdom, the ability to plan and execute; it strengthens courage, perseverance, and character, while calling forth the exercise of tact and skills.

> The special needs of every variety of plant must be studied. Different varieties require different soil and cultivation, and compliance with the laws governing each is the con-

dition of success. The attention required in transplanting, that not even a root fiber shall be crowded or misplaced, the care of the young plants, the pruning and watering, the shielding from frost at night and sun by day, keeping out weeds, disease, and insect pests, the training and arranging, not only teach important lessons concerning the development of character, but the work itself is a means of development. In cultivating carefulness, patience, attention to detail, obedience to law, it imparts a most essential training. The constant contact with the mystery of life and the loveliness of nature, as well as the tenderness called forth in ministering to these beautiful objects of God's creation, tends to quicken the mind and refine and elevate the character; and the lessons taught prepare the worker to deal more successfully with other minds.
Education, 111, 112

Practical work encourages close observation and independent thought. Rightly performed, it tends to develop that practical wisdom which we call common sense. It develops ability to plan and execute, strengthens courage and perseverance, and calls for the exercise of tact and skill.
Ibid., p. 220

She further sees agriculture's role in contributing to purity, contentment, and a living connection with God.

In itself the beauty of nature leads the soul away from sin and worldly attractions, and toward purity, peace, and God. *Counsels to Parents, Teachers, and Students*, 186

Ellen White is far from being an isolated voice in extolling the value of agriculture in the purposeful education of the human race. Hill and Struermann, in *Roots in the Soil,* present as their major concern that the complex superstructure of a technological civilization rests upon the group of workers who handle the soil and deal with nature's resources. They claim:

Discipline, patience, obedience, responsibility and self-reliance are among the morally worthy traits the farmer's mission engenders in him. (Johnson D. Hill and Walter E.

> Struermann, *Roots in the Soil,* New York, 1964, Philosophical Library, 21.)

Even more recently, Anne Moffatt ("Therapy in Plants," *Science Digest*, February 1980, 62, 65) suggests four positive results of gardening and landscaping:
   a. Builds confidence, purpose, and a sense of accomplishment.
   b. Builds respect for living things.
   c. Offers exercise and tangible rewards for efforts.
   d. Offers opportunity for planning, budgeting time, and developing responsibility.

Anne Moffatt (*Ibid.*, *64, 65)* also points out that health care personnel have discovered that gardening:
   a. Helps release tension.
   b. Improves self-esteem and builds ego.
   c. Teaches new skills.
   d. Offers a channel for self-expression.

Karl Menninger, the renowned Kansas psychiatrist, maintained,

> As far as mental health is concerned, farmers have it all over city dwellers. (B.H. Hall; M.E. Kenworthy; "A Psychologist's World," *The Selected Papers of Karl Menninger, M.D.*, 1959, New York, Viking Press, 11.)

It is reasonable to assume that prior to the industrialization of large segments of the world, little attention was given to the extraordinary role of agriculture in the harmonious development of mankind. After all, it is hard to perceive of anything being extraordinary which is the lot (some no doubt felt, the bane) of almost all members of the human race. Thus it is primarily in recent history that the retreat from the soil has been considered a major factor in the great fractures seen in contemporary society. Whereas small farms, with their attendant close-knit family and social units, once covered the expanse of arable America; except for the Amish and their like, the small farm is gone and huge landholdings dominate. Thus millions have been robbed of the helpful and therapeutic value of gardening.

In 1907, addressing the students and faculty of Michigan State University, on the fiftieth anniversary of the founding of the first state-sponsored agricultural college, President Theodore Roosevelt said:

> Our school system has hitherto been well-nigh wholly lacking on the side of industrial training, of the training that fits the men for the shop. . . . Agricultural colleges and farmers' institutes have done much in instruction and inspiration; they have stood for the nobility of labor and the necessity of keeping the muscle and the brain in training for industry. (T heodore Roosevelt, "The Man Who Works With His Hands," *Agricultural Thought in the Twentieth Century*, ed. George McGovern, 1967, The Bobbs-Merrill Co., Inc., 27–32.)

Significantly, Roosevelt's statement has become a watch-cry to some advocates of the critical role for agriculture in education.

> The best crop is the crop of children, the best products of the farm are the men and women raised thereon.
> *Ibid.*, 32

For example, this is Hill and Struermann's claim:

> The chief product of the farms and of agriculture is persons. Hill & Struermann, 22

Perhaps the most convincing evidence for agriculture in the educational curriculum, ironically, does not come from regular classroom investigation. Rather, it comes from the increasing evidence of success with the physically handicapped, the mentally retarded, the emotionally disturbed, the hardened criminal, and the sick.

> As early as 1768, the renowned Philadelphian physician, Benjamin Rush, maintained that digging in the soil could cure the mentally ill. In the nineteenth century, Dr. Gregory, of northern Scotland, claimed cure for insanity by compelling patients to do farm work. (Jody Gaylin, "Green-Thumb for the Handicapped," *Psychology Today*, April 1976, 118.)

> Probably the longest continuous use of horticultural therapy is thought to be the Friends Hospital in Philadelphia, which has used this therapy since its foundation in 1813.
> Moffatt, 65

The effectiveness of gardening in the restoration of the ill and the maladaptive seems to be compelling. Major claims include:

1. Positive results for stroke and accident victims, as well as sufferers of degenerative diseases. (Gaylin, op. cit.)
2. Improvement in mental retardation victims. (*Ibid.*)
3. Some success with bitter and apathetic patients. (*Ibid.*)
4. Improvement in psychiatric patients. (Moffatt, op. cit., 62.)
5. Development of self-worth in teenagers. (*Ibid.*)
6. Reduction of fear in child patients facing operations. (Jack Horn, "The Green-Thumb Care for Hospital Fears," *Psychology Today*, 99.)
7. Aid to senior citizens to realize continued usefulness. (Moffatt, op. cit.)
8. Reaching the psychologically dangerous criminal. (Coralee Leon, "Earth, The Healing Power of Gardening," *House and Garden*, February 1976, 67.)

With this rapidly increasing evidence, and with the spread of hortitherapy, agriculture, and garden therapy, the question which confronts the Christian educator is, What role in prevention does agriculture play? Has the obvious fragmentation of Western society been in part a result of the retreat from the soil? The answer is a resounding, Yes! The introduction of agriculture (or gardening) into the curriculum, as a continuing basic core subject, must be urgently addressed.

Dr. Howard Brook of the Institute of Rehabilitation Medicine in New York said,

> Gardening is preventative medicine—the kind you can prescribe for yourself.
> *Ibid.*

However, is it more than medicine? The pursuits of the soil

offer a broad basis for the development of those human characteristics which are essential for the healthy growth of the individual and the stability of society. While the evidence at hand may not yet be conclusive in the ultimate sense, it is indeed impelling, and thoroughly confirming of God's counsel. First, there is the abundant socio-psychological evidence of an insecure and fragile society, which is generally far removed from its roots in the soil. In contemporary society, the evidence of the dependency syndrome is increasingly apparent. Then, there is the almost irrefutable proof of the success of soil pursuits in human rehabilitation.

Obviously, out-of-doors gardening offers the widest range of benefits for the participants. These benefits include moderate exercise of the major muscle systems of the body, sunshine, and fresh air (except if undertaken in an urbanized area). Not only are these important to physical health, but also to mental and spiritual health.

> Useful occupation was appointed [Adam and Eve] as a blessing, to strengthen the body, to expand the mind, and to develop the character. *Education*, 21

However, where climatic or physical reasons make outdoor gardening impossible, the care of indoor plants or plants in the greenhouse may still have considerable therapeutic and preventive value. Dealing with the therapeutic area, Anne Moffatt says,

> The unique satisfaction derived from getting one's hands into the soil—preparing ground, sowing seeds, observing and nurturing growth, reaping harvests and even pulling weeds seems to frequently set the stage for recovery.
> Moffatt, 62, 63

But she further points out that the single largest group to benefit from garden therapy is the home gardeners. She identified three valuable antidotes to stress in home gardening: exercise, relaxation, and esthetic enjoyment. *Ibid.*, 65

With such wide-ranging benefits to be derived from agricultural pursuits, a strong case can surely be made for the inclusion of agriculture and plant sciences in the core curricula of every school at all levels of education, kindergarten through college. These are based upon God's counsel.

1 *Physical Benefits.* Agriculture, along with many other practical and beneficial pursuits, has much advantage over sports, especially team sports. Physical education experts have increasingly recognized the general failure of team sports to establish lifetime patterns of exercise. Gardening offers a lifetime of such beneficial exercise.

2 *Intellectual Benefits.* When the early investigators of intelligence began their work, the emphasis was directed toward defining intelligence as a general, inherent, cognitive capacity. However, more recent theorists and investigators no longer accept such a simplistic definition of intelligence. Most educators see a wide range of inherent and acquired factors. Of greatest importance to this book is the increasing emphasis upon practical skills, as an index of intelligence, alongside the verbal, numerical, and theoretical reasoning skills.

For example, Vernon years ago defined two major factors of intelligence (verbal–educational and kinestheticmechanical). The continued ability to sustain the practical factors along with the theoretical factors leads to the conclusion that theory and application must stand together in good educational practice. While agriculture is by no means the only worthwhile practical skill, it is surely a skill which, more than most skills, accommodates the wide range of intellectual capacity of mankind; and therefore, it should occupy a primary role in applied education.

3 *Emotional Benefits.* We have yet failed to appreciate fully the devastating psychological effects of the entertainment syndrome upon modern culture. This failure not only dominates our leisure-time activities, but has invaded education, work, the church, and almost all phases of life.

It is just now that we are beginning to realize the destructive psychological effect of living a life built largely around vicarious experiences. Most children and adults have spent thousands of hours in the make-believe experience of television and other entertainment media, while spending little time in their self-initiated experience. Agriculture activities offer an excellent antidote to such mental health hazards.

The experiences in the real world, the basic cause-and-effect lessons, and the personal fulfillment of agriculture, must help preserve mental health and offer experiences in meeting the real issues of life. These lessons significantly contribute to the establishment of self-worth.

4 *Spiritual Benefits.* The moral benefits of hard work and worthwhile pursuits have long been recognized. The accomplishment of productive tasks and the rewards of honest labor sustain a platform for growth, which will facilitate the choice of the worthwhile and the valuable. Idleness, indolence, and failure to achieve worthwhile ends not only threaten the emotional health of an individual, but also predispose the individual to antisocial and often criminal behavior. Agriculture, along with other worthwhile practical programs, can facilitate sound moral and spiritual growth.

While it is not within the scope of this chapter to detail the way agriculture might most effectively be integrated into the school curricula, a number of observations may be helpful as is detailed in the summary.

SUMMARY

1 Whenever possible, schools should have sufficient land so that every student may have a small garden of his or her own for which to care. Health institutions should provide opportunity for garden therapy.
2 It may be advisable to have some opportunity for group agricultural pursuits, where such social intercourse would be deemed advisable. This would be helpful for educational and health institutions.
3 The success of such programs is postulated upon teachers and health workers engaging in and helping the students and health guests in their gardens.
4 Where there is much cold weather, greenhouses should be provided for the students' or health guests' gardening program.

5 Gardening courses should offer increasing levels of scientific understanding, as well as practical experience.
6 Experimentation with soil enrichment and food quality analysis might also be added in some institutions.
7 Agriculture should stand beside Bible reading, English, writing, mathematical and spiritual training, as the core of any educational curriculum. True Christian education will offer every opportunity for students to gain an education in the pursuits of the soil.

Chapter 14

Choosing Property

SELECTING a property is not a minor decision. There are factors which have been divinely mandated and other factors which common sense and informed counsel will help. The main divinely mandated and common sense principles are:

1   A training institution must be located in the country on sufficient land to provide a high measure of privacy and suitability for establishing the necessary operating buildings and housing. There should be adequate arable land for the production of as much food as will provide for most of the needs of the institution.

> It seems strange to everybody that we should be located in the woods. But we do not want our students to be near the city. We know that even though we bring them into the country we cannot escape from all evil. . . . But in the country the youth are away from the sights and the sounds of the city. We desire to take the students away from the foul atmosphere of the city. Not that Satan is not here. He is here, but we are trying to do all we can to place the students in the very best circumstance in order that they may fasten their eyes on Christ.   *Manuscript Releases*, Vol. 11, 158

> Let the students be out in the most healthful location that can be secured, to do the very work that should have been done years ago. Then there would not be such great discouragements. Had this been done, you would have had some grumbling from students, and many objections would have been raised by parents, but this all-around education would prepare children and youth not only for

practical work in various trades, but would fit them for the Lord's farm in the earth made new. If all in America had encouraged the work in agricultural lines that principals and teachers have discouraged, the schools would have had altogether a different showing.

There is room within earth's vast boundaries for schools to be located where ground can be cleared, land cultivated, and where a proper education can be given. This work is essential for an all-round education, and one which is favorable to spiritual advancement. Nature's voice is the voice of Jesus Christ, teaching us innumberable lessons of perseverance. The mountains and the hills are changing, the earth is waxing old like a garment, but the blessing of God, which spreads a table for his people in the wilderness, will never cease.

The Paulson Collection, Sept. 24, 1898

2 It is important to check carefully with the county authorities in the U.S.A. or other local government authorities in countries outside the United States, concerning whether there are any liens against the property. No one can afford to have such surprises after they have purchased the property. When we were reviewing Hartland Hall Plantation as a likely location for Hartland Institute we learned that the Madison County court had ruled that no liens could be placed against the future purchaser of the property. That was most important to us.

3 In this day and age where environmentalist issues are strong, it is wise to check in advance concerning any possible environmental problems. Often, as environmentalists are rapidly extending their reach and influence upon legislators, more care must be taken in this area. It can be an extraordinarily expensive proposition for a property to be found to be in any way in violation of environmental laws. This situation could lead to very expensive cleanup operations. While Christians should have a desire to support worthwhile environmental principles, it would certainly be foolish to purchase a property which has environmental problems. We have a friend who had to expend tens of thousands of dollars to clean up toxic waste materials.

4 Another important issue is soil percolation ability and county regulations concerning the installation and use of septic tanks. Constructing, as we have had to do at Hartland, a full septic system and sewage ponds to meet all the environmental criteria is quite expensive; and it is an ongoing expense to have regular testing and monitoring of the discharge to meet state requirements. In most jurisdictions sewage ponds require expensive lining which must be replaced every twenty or thirty years.

5 It should be possible to obtain a soil map of the property. That soil map will provide you with some idea of the quality of soil and the arability of the land. This is important for farming purposes. We had available from the beginning a soil map of Hartland Institute. It is like a patchwork quilt with some very good davidson soil, and some very poor soil such as blackjack.

6 Does the property have a good natural water supply? Keep in mind that if the property which is being considered has been a private property it cannot be taken for granted that the rules which pertain for a private property are the same for those of an institution. For example, you may be assured that there is a wonderful water supply. However, in Virginia, where Hartland Institute is located, no water can be accessed for an institution less than fifty feet below the surface That is, the well has to be cased (to keep out possibly contaminated ground water) for a minimum of fifty feet. Colin recalls that when digging one well they found abundance of water at about twenty feet, but that did not meet the criterion of depth for an institution. However, a private owner could have chosen to case to twenty feet and use the water.

   Make sure that existing wells meet the criteria of the state in which the proposed institution is located. It is also wise to check the bacterial level in the water, which can easily be accomplished through state agencies in the region. It is essential also to conduct a twenty-four-hour test of water flow. The history of water supply in the region is also very important. Question whether in droughts the water supply fails. Estimation should be made of the amount of water the institution will require for future institute populations. Is the flow adequate?

There is a need to make allowance for the additional water needs when convocations, camp meetings or seminars are held. If there is a stream running through or bounding the property, enquiry should be made as to the riparian rights which would permit the use of water from such waterways for agricultural or other purposes. If the property possesses a stream with sufficient drop in elevation to allow for a small hydroelectric station to be built, that would be well worth exploring.

7   County building codes can vary greatly from one county to another and from one state to another. Some places in the United States have no building codes or very minor codes. Others have very demanding codes. The more regulations, keep in mind, the greater will be the cost of building. But the buildings erected are likely to be of a superior quality. Also there may be considerable risks concerning significant restrictions in building *per se*. At Hartland we have seen a decided increase in building regulations. Of course it is not possible to foresee the future in purchasing property, but every new regulation costs money. Other institutions could see restrictions added as we have faced, or will face, in the near future, requiring the development of a sewage system, the installation of a large tower for water containment, the providing of three-phase electricity, an added requirement of environmental impact studies and, as population increases, the requirement to provide special access and exit lanes from the county road into the property.

8   Obtain written statements from the county to confirm the property is zoned to carry on the ministry which you propose to fulfill.

9   Cost of transportation. An institute must keep in mind that increasingly its staff will be travelling to a wide range of speaking appointments and activities. The further the distance to mass transit facilities, the greater the operation costs to the institution. Remember the kind of institution you

are planning. If, like Hartland, you have a college, wellness center, publishing house and many meetings on the campus, the distance will translate into large amounts of dollars. Our closest bus station is about eight miles away, the closest train station is about twelve miles away, the closest commuter airport is thirty-seven miles away and the closest interstate and international airport is almost seventy miles away. It is estimated to cost over thirty cents a mile to operate a car; hundreds of trips each year translate into many thousands of dollars.

10 Shopping Facilities. It is very difficult for staff and students if shopping centers are too far away from the institution. In the case of Hartland we have reasonable shopping centers eight and twelve miles away and very good shopping centers forty miles away. The shopping center twelve miles away can provide for most needs, it having a Wal-Mart super store and Lowe's among quite a number of other store options. Once again, if the institution is in a remote area, there is a great hardship and cost in travelling to the closest suitable shopping area.

11 The Cost of Property. Clearly property in the United States, as with any country, varies greatly according to the general locale in which the property is situated. Because it is required that a good sized acreage should be purchased, cost becomes very important. Rarely would it be profitable to sacrifice acreage in order to afford considerably higher per acre cost of the land. Hartland has seven hundred and sixty-one acres. Originally we bought seven hundred and sixty-five acres, but four acres was ceded to the county on the agreement that they would widen the road for over one and a half miles from Highway 15 to the eastern end of our property. That was a deal which we thought advantageous to Hartland and so it has proven.

12 We have counsel that under the providences of God it will be possible to find properties which have sufficient buildings upon them to commence operations quickly. These will be available well below their market value thus permitting a quick commencement to the institution.

Let men of sound judgment be appointed, not to publish abroad their intentions, but to search for such properties in the rural districts, in easy access to the cities, suitable for small training schools for workers, and where facilities may also be provided for treating the sick and weary souls who know not the truth. Look for such places just out from the large cities, where suitable buildings may be secured, either as a gift from the owners, or purchased at a reasonable price by the gifts of our people. Do not erect buildings in the noisy cities.   *Medical Ministry,* 308, 309

The Lord will work upon human minds in unexpected quarters. Some who apparently are enemies of the truth will, in God's providence, invest their means to develop properties and erect buildings. In time these properties will be offered for sale at a price far below their cost. Our people will recognize the hand of Providence in these offers and will secure valuable property for use in educational work. They will plan and manage with humility, self-denial, and self-sacrifice. Thus men of means are unconsciously preparing auxiliaries that will enable the Lord's people to advance His work rapidly.
Testimonies, Vol. 7, 102

As we have mentioned before, the faster an institution can begin, the better will be the support and interest in the project. The property which we purchased had a very large mansion and ten homes upon it. While this was by no means all the buildings which we needed, nevertheless it was sufficient to start the first college year and then, months later, we began the wellness center, which was soon followed by Hartland Publications.

13   Occasionally it may be possible to take over an existing self-supporting property. This can be more than simply a pipe dream. In the last couple of decades a number of self-supporting facilities have become available. By law the assets of defunct non-profit organizations must be donated to another non-profit corporation. This means that if a self-supporting property is closing, for whatever reason, it may be possible to negotiate to take over such a property providing you can obtain a non-profit corporation status or already have one. In rare cases you can negotiate to take over the institution as it is, including its non-profit status. In the last thirty years a number of self-supporting institutions have closed or changed hands. These include Groveland in Florida, for many years a very successful family-operated educational institution. As the founders grew old there was no one to take their place. Eventually it changed hands. Beautiful Valley Institute in West Virginia closed down. The same happened to Alpine Springs Academy in Wisconsin. It had functioned very successfully for some time. In Mississippi for many years Pine Forest Academy and Sanitarium functioned very successfully, the academy being headed by an educator and the health center being operated by his physician brother. For all intents and purposes for many years Cherry Hill Institute closed down although it is now functioning on a very limited scale.

14 Land slippage is an important factor, especially in undulating or hilly properties. The local government authorities should be able to provide you with this information.

To check out the possible availability of a faltering self-supporting institution it would be wise to check with Outpost Centers Incorporated, 5340 Layton Lane, Apison, Tennessee, 37302; phone 423-236-5600, email info@outpostcenters.org, and Association of Services and Industry, contact the director at the North American Division of the General Conference headquarters at 301-680-6000, or the Layman's Foundation, P. O. Box 747, Ooltewah, Tennessee, 37363, phone 615-238-5537 or 615-690-7717.

SUMMARY

1 Divine Counsel.
    a. Establish an outpost center in a rural location.
    b. Select a property with many buildings already erected upon it which is available well below its market value.

    c. There must be suitable land for operating a farm and establishing other industries.
2. Other considerations:
    a. Make sure that there are no liens against the property before purchase.
    b. Check carefully to be assured that there are no major environmental concerns to deal with on the property.
    c. Does the property have significant areas of soil with good percolation?
    d. Check to see if you can obtain a soil map of the property.
    e. Does the county permit the use of septic tanks upon the property?
    f. Does the property have a good permanent water supply?
    g. Check the depth of any wells on the property.
    h. Check the twenty-four hour water flow from the wells.
    i. What is the history of the well's production in prolonged periods of drought?
    j. If it is possible to develop a hydroelectric station on the property that would be a decided plus.
    k. Is the water supply sufficient for large gatherings to take place?
    l. Check carefully the county building codes.
    m. Make sure the country permits buildings and operations for all that is planned to be accomplished at the Institute.
    n. Check out the proximity of the property to major public transportation.
    o. Check how far the property is from adequate shopping areas.
    p. Check the cost of properties in different regions of the country and also the evaluation of properties in the county you are considering.
    q. Check with OCI, Layman's Foundation or ASI to determine if there is any property available where a

Choosing Property

ministry has ceased to function which might be available for your ministry.

r. Visit the county seat and determine the level of slippage of the land where building construction is proposed.

Chapter 15
Developing the Physical Plant

AS is stated in the chapter entitled "Choosing a Property," it is not wise to purchase a property on which there are no existing buildings. However, should there be no physical plant, or at the best very little and much less than is needed even to commence an institution, this situation does provide a splendid opportunity to build facilities that are most effective for the early needs of the institution. However, count the cost in advance. Here are a number of pointers.

1   It is a great help from the beginning to devise a campus plan. This plan should seek to design the locating of anticipated future buildings. Keep in mind that major administrative buildings should be in close proximity to each other and yet not so designed that it will appear that the campus is cluttered. Esthetics do matter! Homes for staff need to be sufficiently separated from each other so that the staff members do not believe they are living in a mini-city. Yet one has also to keep in mind that certain residential areas, if properly designed and located, will reduce costs.

   The cost of running utilities to various parts of the campus is very expensive if homes are too widely separated from each other. Each home must be provided with water and electricity lines and, if it is required or desired to have sewage treatment ponds, then the home must be connected to the sewage system. If the property is undulating it should not be forgotten that buildings built at lower elevations may require sewage pumps to pump the sewage. This will not only add to capital investment but also to additional operating costs. Beside buildings, major farm lands and gardens should be located in specific areas of the campus, taking into account soil quality and water access. The advice of a local agriculturist will be helpful here. If plans are laid to erect greenhouses, the sites of these should also be placed in the master plan. The industrial segment of the campus should be located some distance from Administrative and residential areas, but not built so far away as to incur huge costs in providing electricity, water and sewage connections.

Hartland had the volunteer services, in its early days, of a fine campus planner in Dr. Ray Davidson from Andrews University. The development which has taken place at Hartland has followed that master plan with very few alterations. It has been a great blessing to have that plan in place. It is wise in the initial stages of the institution to share the master plan envisaged by the Board with the county building inspector so that there are no great surprises as to the institute's development. Under these circumstances, it will be easier to introduce the building inspector to any new buildings of the future. The Master plan should indicate that as the institute develops, there may be significant changes to the plan. Counties are pleased when there is a systematic and well-thought-out plan in advance.

2   Seek to find an architect who well understands self-supporting work. It may be possible to find an architect who will volunteer his services or, alternatively, charge a much reduced fee. We emphasize the necessity to find someone who understands self-supporting work because he will realize that while the buildings must be attractive, they must above all be functional, while avoiding unnecessary costs and elaborate decorations. Always keep in mind that the design originally chosen should set the style for an onward developing building program. Few aspects of an institution are more unattractive than buildings of strikingly different architectural design. Remember the need for harmony and unity of design for the buildings. This will enhance the beauty of the campus and ultimately will reduce cost. Hartland was very grateful for the services of a very fine architectural firm

from the Northwest, Don Kirkman Associates, who designed our Wellness Center. Its design complemented the southern mansion already on the property when it was purchased.

3 Especially in the early years of development, it is likely that volunteers will make themselves available to contribute to the building program of an institution. However, there are some drawbacks. It is essential to ascertain that the volunteers have proven track records and expertise in the building areas they are undertaking. It is not always easy to attract volunteers in all the major building areas. We were grateful for some competent retired or semi-retired, as well as active tradesmen who continued to help us. Bill Perry, a very fine electrician; Lynwood Spangler, a master plumber, who, with his wife and team did all the ground level plumbing for the Wellness Center, were extremely valuable volunteers. Later Lynwood became a Hartland student, graduating from the Pastoral Evangelism major. He is now an ordained minister and an evangelist presently serving in the Texas Conference. We had quality carpenters volunteer, including Jim Collins, and volunteers with experience in drywall. Bob Logan, from Oregon, an expert in heavy equipment operation, was a mighty help to us. He did much of the early backhoe and bulldozer work. Many other volunteers continue to bless Hartland. As this manuscript is completed, many volunteers are helping with the construction of the new young ladies dormitories. Keep in mind however, the important opportunity to use construction and maintainance projects as excellent training experience for young people.

A little more difficult for us was to find someone skilled in heating and cooling, but we did obtain help. Of course, other volunteers with some expertise can also contribute, under the guidance of specialist tradesmen. However, there needs to be an experienced project manager and, if possible, that person should be part of the resident staff. He needs to be a man who will guarantee the integrity of the design and the quality of the workmanship.

There are organizations which can be a help. Some will bring a team for up to a couple of weeks or even longer and

Developing the Physical Plant

accomplish a significant amount of work in the construction area. Maranatha Flights International is one of the best known examples, but not the only one. We had the privilege of Maranatha Flights International assisting us in the early stages of the building of the Wellness Center. In spite of the inclement weather most of the time that they were present, they accomplished much, for which we owe them a debt of gratitude. However, it is better to wait to find expert help, rather than go ahead with those who do not have sufficient expertise, and who may make very serious mistakes which will prove very costly and bring heartbreak later. There is a role for less skilled volunteer laborers and these are a blessing but the volunteer tradesmen must be experienced.

4   Those involved in building projects must seek to fulfill all county and state building requirements. To be discovered breaking the county codes brings discredit upon the institution and may eventually lead to rejection of future projects. We must show ourselves to be responsible and law-abiding citizens.

5   It should not be overlooked that building codes continue to alter and that those changes, if not adhered to, can add to the cost of buildings. We cite one example. At Hartland we had been authorized to build a certain number of homes without applying for new permits. We had laid the foundation of a new home without the knowledge that new, much stricter, standards had been put in place. We faced the added cost of taking up the foundations we had already put in place and then replacing them with the foundations which met the new code. Thus even when permission of the county has been granted to go ahead with new buildings, should an extended period of time elapse before starting, contact the county building department to inquire if there has been any change in the building code.

6   Remember that states now have increasingly strong environmental codes. Keep closely in touch with the requirements of those codes and seek to fulfill them conscientiously.

7   Keep close to the county building inspector. Earn his trust and that will solve a huge number of difficulties in

the future. Keep in mind that new building inspectors may be appointed. Do not expect a new inspector to have the same confidence in you which the previous inspector had. It is likely that the new building inspector will be younger, sometimes beginning his first administrative post in this role, especially if you are located in a smaller county. It has been Colin's experience that younger and newer building inspectors are tougher than those who have had many years of experience. Building inspectors will, from time to time, attend conferences with inspectors from much larger counties and large cities where the codes are, by necessity, much more demanding than in most small rural areas. They may return from these conferences with a determination to meet some of these more rigid codes which will add costs to the project. Thus the person in charge of the building programs should be an individual who can build up a reputation for integrity and honesty and therefore gain the respect and cooperation of the building inspector. Acrimonious arguing is not an option for Christians.

8 In deciding upon a building, make it a little larger than your present needs. However do not make the mistake of constructing it significantly larger than these needs. If you design the building well, you will allow for expansion of the building if this is needed in the future expansion of the institute. This counsel applies to student dormitories, small wellness centers or publishing houses. No institution can be assured of large and rapid growth. Some leaders are super optimists, and while our vision should not be limited to narrow goals and purposes, nevertheless conservatism in what we build will exhibit fiscal responsibility.

9 Remember that every square foot which is added to the size of the building will engender significant costs. These costs will be limited not only to the building itself. Increase in size will also raise costs in areas such as flooring, lighting and many other fixed and movable assets in each room. Some of these costs, such as lighting, cooling or heating will be ongoing, thus placing a drain upon operating expenses.

10 As we have noted in point (9) above, overbuilding will not only increase the cost of capital expenditure, it will result in a considerable increase in operating expenses. We quote a rule of thumb. Whatever a building has cost to erect and equip, will require an expenditure of about five percent of that cost to operate annually. That is to say that operational budget will have to be increased by approximately five percent of the capital cost of the building, furnishings and equipment annually. For example, if a building costs one hundred thousand dollars to construct, it will add approximately five thousand dollars to the institution's operating budget per annum. Thus over a twenty-year period the institution will have expended approximately the same costs to operate the building as it cost to erect the building. That is a significant increase. What are some of those costs? They include repairs and maintenance, depreciation, insurance and taxes (if applicable), lighting, heating, cooling and other utility costs, janitorial work and staffing costs. Thus before a building is designed these costs need to be factored into the operating budget. Every square foot saved on a building will save operational expenses in the years ahead. Of course we are not advocating developing plans so spartan that the building lacks adequate functionality. However, the operating costs must be carefully weighed before the size of a building is determined. There are administrators who judge their achievements according to the construction of new buildings. Buildings have their place, but they are not the final evaluation of the effectiveness of an institution nor its leader.

11 It is the quality and success of ministry above everything else which defines the degree of success of the institution and the administration. Generally speaking it is better to have the funds in hand before undertaking a new building. At the present phase of Hartland's development we seek to have at least a major proportion of the funds in hand before we commence a new necessary building project. In the past, only on one occasion did we borrow money to build. That was for the construction of the Wellness Center. However, we followed the counsel of the Lord that if we were to borrow we should borrow from "friends of the enterprise."

> That our schools may nobly accomplish the purpose for which they are established, they should be free from debt. They should not be left to bear the burden of paying interest. In the establishment of training schools for workers, and especially in new fields where the brethren are few and their means limited, rather than delay the work it may be better to hire some money from the friends of the enterprise; but whenever it is possible, let our institutions be dedicated free from debt. *Testimonies*, Vol. 6, 207

Bethel Sanitarium in southern Indiana graciously loaned three hundred thousand dollars to finish the health center. Colin was not favorable to this loan and voted against accepting it. However, the wisdom of the board proved much greater than his wisdom, and God blessed the decision and we were able to retire the debt in a timely fashion, with additional generosity from Bethel Sanitarium.

The final counsel we would offer is to build for necessity, not as a memorial to some human being.

SUMMARY

1. Early in the project, set out a campus plan including location of
   a. Main administration and institute ministry buildings.
   b. Industrial and vocational buildings.
   c. Staff and student home area.
   d. Agriculture and garden area.
   e. Greenhouses.
2. The plan should take into account the costs of running water, sewage and electrical lines.
3. Buildings will be more attractive if there is architectural harmony in the buildings erected.
4. Build functional, well constructed buildings, attractive but not elaborate.
5. Seek quality, experienced volunteer help.
6. It is wise that, if possible, the project manager be a staff member.

Developing the Physical Plant

7. Make sure you know well and follow the county building codes. Remember that these codes change from time to time, so do nothing without rechecking.
8. Especially make sure you are aware of the environmental protection laws.
9. Develop a respectful relationship with the building inspector. Keep him updated on decisions and change of plans.
10. Be careful not to over-build, always remembering the additional capital costs, and that it costs about five percent of the building cost to operate the building annually.
11. Do not under-build for this could greatly reduce the building's usefulness.
12. Where possible, build in such a way that later expansion, if necessary, can be undertaken.
13. Do not incur large debt for building. Seek to raise most of the money before the construction is commenced.
14. If it is necessary to borrow, borrow from a friend of the institution.

Chapter 16

Financing a New Project

IT is one thing to have a vision and a passion for establishing a new self-supporting institution. It is altogether a different matter to have gathered sufficient start-up funds to provide a basis for success. The most valuable asset which may be had, beside the providential leadership of the Lord, is an experienced and proven successful leader. At the very first meeting of the interim board of directors of the institution which became Hartland Institute, a leader was chosen. Colin was that leader. Only rarely a leader may be found who has as much administrative experience as Colin possessed. He had been the president of two colleges, the chairman of the Education Department of another college and had been the founding dean of Weimar College. This background experience served to provide Hartland with a very important profile, for he was well known in both denominational and self-supporting circles. Later we will discuss leadership. Suffice here to say that the choice of a leader is critical to fundraising success as well as to the establishment of sound operating procedures. However do not be daunted by the challenge of finding the finest leader available. The leader must always exert a strong hand in fund raising, but above all he must be one who has a deep knowledge of God's truth and institutional principles, and resolute firmness to stand unwaveringly for divine principles.

It is similarly crucial to attract a fine staff. Some who comprised the original staff of Hartland were very well known, tested and tried individuals. From the very commencement of the institution three physicians, three nurses, two doctorates

Financing a New Project

in health science, one respiratory therapist, and one dietician were available for the health program. The opportunity of having such a qualified team with which to begin is rare. But then, when the Institution was first proposed, the founders of Hartland had not expected to commence with such a team. The college appointed a well-known academy Bible teacher, the former head of the Health Department of Weimar College and one of his associates. Also of great strength was the appointed Director of Development who had served as the Associate Director of the Temperance Department of the General Conference. He also served as the college outreach director.

There can be no doubt that those who were evaluating this new institution, making decisions to support its work, were influenced by the experience of the team. Also, the initial board was able to attract very well known and influential personnel, some who themselves gave liberally to the new institution. At an early stage, Hartland's board of directors included five Union ASI leaders. Yet above all these important considerations were the fervent prayers of consecrated men and women who had surrendered all to the ministry of the Lord.

Even with all these advantages, the first year was a tremendous test of faith, and the first ten years were beset with many financial challenges. Now if listening to this you are inclined to be discouraged, think not of it. If God is calling for a new institution to be established for His glory and the hastening of His coming, nothing can stop it, for God is in control as He has ever been at Hartland Institute.

> If God be for us, who can be against us?
>
> Romans 8:31

Yet it will take wisdom, along with faith, for any institution to prove successful and much of that wisdom will come in financial management. The ingredient of faith, when faced with seemingly insurmountable difficulties, is the greatest need. Faith will lead to miracles, genuine miracles. But be assured the staff will be sorely tested in this domain. Satan is not inactive when yet another fortress of truth and righteousness is being established. Your extremity will be God's opportunity. Keep in mind, however, that you will almost certainly not have all the resources necessary to start an institution. In the beginning, faith will enter into the equation and God will call you to take those steps of faith. We believe that whomever God is calling to commence such an institution will be those to whom He has provided opportunities for experience in a wide range of situations.

Those who have been well trained in self-supporting work at a self-supporting institution will be more likely at an earlier age to begin such a new project successfully. For example, it has been our vision to encourage institutions to commence in many different parts of the world by training six to eight young people from regions in the world in various disciplines so that as a team they can return to their home region and begin such an institution. In most instances it is difficult to achieve this number. It is best if those young people have the opportunity to have spent time as well in other institutions so they can understand the modus operandi of at least one other successful institution. A number of former staff members from Hartland have set up their own self-supporting institutions. The experience they have gathered over a number of years on the staff at Hartland has been invaluable to their success in these ministries.

It is very difficult to finance an institution without being well known. It is a great help to attract experienced preachers and health educators associated with the planning and promoting of a new institution. Such can seek speaking appointments far and wide in order to spread the word concerning the upcoming institution. These can collect names and addresses to form the basis of a mailing address list, to distribute material explaining the institute, and encourage people to support it. We have found it not necessary to limit such activities to the immediate region where the institution is located. If people gain a vision of an institution which is planning to do the kind of work which they themselves see important, it is then likely that they will seriously consider financially supporting it. However, you will always face the fact that there will be those who will be cautious and unlikely to help any institution until there is sufficient evidence that it really is going to mature and be a long term project for the Lord. The more adventuresome folk will likely be attracted to an exciting new venture. But keep in mind that these initial donors may not always be long-term donors. Once the institution is established they may look for a new institute to support. However, there are those who will support the initial stages and maintain that support continually thereafter.

Wise leaders will not only look to attract new supporters, but to retain previous supporters. This can be achieved only by information that clearly chronicles the results of an active ministry. It is most important to set forth evidence in the initial planning stage, and before the institution has officially commenced, that much effective outreach work is being accomplished. Support will increase, and confidence will be strengthened, if those who know about the institution also have the opportunity to be assured that soul-winning activities are taking place. Place needs regularly before the donors. This takes a level of balance. On the one hand it is wise to present more than one focus for different projects which appeal to different minds. However, be careful not to have so many projects at any one time that none of them may be accomplished, which can lead to confusion in the minds of potential donors. Above all, make sure that you not only send a receipt but a thank-you note to your donors. Donors need to know that they are not taken for granted and that they are genuinely appreciated by the institution leaders.

SUMMARY

1   Institutional ministries require sufficient funds so that the ministry will commence quickly after the initial announcements.
2   The choice of a proven or well-known leader is very helpful to the institute's fund raising success.
3   The quality and experience of the staff likewise contrib-

utes to a successful fund-raising campaign.
4. Board members should be carefully chosen, not so much for the size of their potential contribution, but to add strength to the fund raising program.
5. Above all a consecrated heart and constant, earnest prayer will most successfully tap the resources of heaven.
6. Essential is the ingredient of faith in a new venture.
7. Expect divine miracles when you reach your extremity.
8. Training and working in successful self-supporting ministries is an important foundation for commencing a new institute.
9. Scatter your preachers, teachers and health staff to familiarize church members with the project and its needs.
10. Look for those who are willing to support a not-yet-commenced institution, and once the institution has commenced, seek others who now may be willing to add their support to the ministry.
11. Donors need to know they are important to the ministry and are appreciated. Send them letters of gratitude with some special news about the progress of the ministry.

Chapter 17
Developing Financial Support

THERE is no strong, regular financial support independent of a vibrant, effective and actively ongoing ministry. At Hartland Institute we have recognized this and thus we no longer have a financial development division. Rather we have a Stewardship Ministries Division which is designed not only to raise funds for the institute, but to minister to the spiritual needs of supporters and donors. What is the chief purpose of a stewardship ministry division? Sister White is explicit that operation costs of colleges should be provided by charging adequate fees to the students. By extension, the principle will extend to health centers in their charges to health guests. She warned Avondale College leaders, for example, that they had established a fee structure too low and the fees had to be increased so that the college could operate from its own income. However, the other needs of a college and an institute should be supplied by benevolent brethren and sisters.

> In some of our schools the price of tuitions has been too low. This has in many ways been detrimental to the educational work. . . . Whatever may have been the object in placing the tuition at less than a living rate, the fact that a school has been running behind heavily is sufficient reason for reconsidering the plans and arranging its charges so that in the future its showing may be different. The amount charged for tuition, board, and residence should be sufficient to pay the salaries of the faculty, to supply the table with an abundance of healthful, nourishing food, to maintain the furnishing of the rooms, to keep the buildings

in repair, and to meet other necessary running expenses [that is, cover the operating expenses].

Testimonies, Vol. 6, 210, 211

Rather than the financial burden resting upon the college to struggle to operate on an inadequate income, fees should be adequate to provide all college operating needs. However, Sister White recognized that some students, try as they might, will not be able to raise all their fees. Thus she called on church members to support financially these needy students.

> The churches in different localities should feel that a solemn responsibility rests upon them to train youth and educate talent to engage in missionary work. When they see those in the church who give promise of making useful workers, but who are not able to support themselves in the school, they should assume the responsibility of sending them to one of our training schools. . . . There are persons who would do good service in the Lord's vineyard, but many are too poor to obtain without assistance the education that they require. *Ibid.,* 211

> The duty devolves on the church to see that a fund is raised to be appropriated to the education of students who are worthy but have not at their command the means of obtaining an education.
>
> *Manuscript Release No. 21*, 462

Although Sister White does not give counsel on this subject, it may be inappropriate to ask for funds for simple operating costs, except perhaps at the very beginning until the school is well established. Thereafter, donations should be solicited for significant capital needs such as major buildings, major equipment. Stewardship ministries ought also to seek to raise funds for worthy, needy students. Faithful Seventh-day Adventists should be made aware of the needs of such students. At Hartland we call this fund the "Missionary Training Fund," for its purpose is solely to train young men and women for the work of gospel soul saving. Such a fund should be administered very wisely by ensuring that those who are benefiting from the fund are exerting every effort to support themselves, and that their parents and local church members are seeking to help them whenever possible. Thus the order of support is:

1 First, the students themselves. At Hartland College we provide opportunity for students to work in their vacation times. We also encourage our young people to colporteur where they can minister while also seeking to support themselves. A few students are so talented in colporteuring that they can cover their financial needs at college. All to a significant degree are able to support the cost of college tuition room and board.

2 If parents are in a position to help, they should be urged to do so. However, sometimes, especially in the cases of overseas students from developing countries, that is not possible. In other cases where the parents are not sympathetic to their training at Hartland, they may receive nothing at all.

3 Finally, it is left to the benevolent church members to help such needy cases. Sister White is adamant that debt should not be incurred by the institution. She counsels that the church members should rally to the support of the young people who earnestly seek to help themselves narrow the financial gap needed to provide for their education. We must keep in mind that God will have a generation of young people who will bear the heavy burdens when the final message is taken under most difficult circumstances to the world. An investment in dedicated young people is an investment in the hastening of the coming of our Lord and Savior.

The third and very important area for seeking financial help from God's people is to support a wide range of missionary endeavors. These endeavors include evangelism, outreach, health ministries, literature distribution and Bible work. If only a ten-cent piece of literature were to be distributed to every one in China it would cost one hundred and thirty million dollars; to India it would require one hundred and ten million dollars; to Africa almost eighty million dollars; to North and South America seventy-five million dollars. To share such a tract to the rest of Asia and all of Europe would raise the cost to about six hundred and fifty million dollars. Now not every one in the world can read. There are many who will have to hear the living messenger. Almost certainly those who cannot read will have very few electronic devices to hear the message in some other media form. Whatever the difficulty, we may be sure that God will find a way to share the message to the world.

The choice of a stewardship ministry director is one of the key decisions of an institution. Few people have the skills necessary to accomplish both the spiritual and financial goals. It will require a man or woman of great integrity. He or she will have a feel for the whole needs of an institution. More than that, he or she should subordinate his or her own preferences of emphasis to those of the combined wisdom of the institution leaders. It is essential that no one feel left out and that no area be treated partially.

The stewardship leader however needs to discover the preferences which the donors have toward specific projects. Some focus upon student financial help while others choose literature projects. Some will support the development of the physical plant of the institution. Some have a focus upon agricultural needs or industries. The stewardship director, more than anyone else, learns the giving patterns and preferences of the donors. Some donors have a wide range of emphases and are ready to donate wherever there is a need. Thus some donors will not specify that for which the donation is to be given. In such situations it is not the development directors' province to decide where that donation is to be placed. This decision must be accorded to the full administrative team after prayerful consideration.

Because of the sensitive and important financial information which a stewardship ministry director possesses, there are potential problems when such an officer leaves one institution to serve another or maybe to be part of a newly formed institution. Here strict ethical considerations must be followed by the departing stewardship officer. Keep in mind that the stewardship director or anyone closely connected to the financial donation areas is very likely to have wide knowledge of the major donors. It is unethical and illegal to take the donor list from one institution to another without approval from the Institute that owns the list. Even if such permission were granted by the institution whose list it is, there are many who consider that the sharing of the names and contact information of the mailing list is unethical without the individual permission of these people. However, such an officer knows the donor list well and he knows the major donors very well. Even though he may not take the donor list, that does not mean that he will not be in close contact and be likely to attract at least some of the donations of those people to his new organization. Of course, it would be against Scripture and Spirit of Prophecy to take any legal action in this situation and, thus, it would be wrong to do so. Since God is in charge of our institutions, He will find other ways to make up any deficit in support from the transferred giving of such donors. We have certainly found that God has supplied our needs at Hartland in such circumstances.

It takes a humble and deeply committed Christian to fulfill this role because finance, in itself, if not properly handled, offers opportunities for misappropriation. The one chosen must be an individual of impeccable integrity and honesty, a person who will not use his or her personal influence and financial power to seek to dominate institutional decision making. His or her focus must be upon the spiritual nurturing of supporters of the institution. Such an individual will be a safe person to place in the stewardship responsibility.

However, the financial side of the development or stewardship role is not limited to straightforward fund raising. The stewardship leader has a responsibility to learn, if he does not already know them, skills in other areas—in setting up trusts, in helping prepare wills, estate planning, in seeking donations of equipment or property which can be sold to support ministry projects. One has to be careful, however, in receiving properties. Sometimes properties which are difficult to sell or have been poor investments, are eventually donated to self-supporting institutions. Keep in mind that when you accept a property donation you also are accepting the annual property taxes. It is important to discover what they are before accepting the property. Such a property has no value and will, indeed, engender a cost if in a reasonable period of time it is not sold. First seek a private sale to avoid realtor costs. Advertising in denominational papers will sometimes lead to a sale.

Another area for fundraising is among those not of our faith. Some institutions have had very significant donations from the general community of those not of our faith. Some of these have been people blessed through health programs. Sometimes they are members of the community who, for whatever reason, will have shown an interest in the program which is being operated. Hartland has not had a large number of donations from those not of our faith, but it has had some, and some have been quite significant in size. I believe that there is considerable wisdom in seeking donations from the community and also from foundations.

When Russell was President of Bangkok Adventist Hospital, Thailand, (1979-1984), under God's blessing over $U.S.1,500,000 was raised from non-Seventh-day Adventist members of the public towards the $U.S. 2,000,000 cost of the erection of the Ralph Waddell Wing. God surely blessed. Almost all the donations came from Thai citizens who were Buddhists.

Any institution, especially a Christian institution, must seek to provide evidence of fiscal responsibility. It is not unusual for self-supporting institutions to reach financially difficult times. Proper handling of such situations is critical. Immediately suspend any expenditures for activities which are non-revenue producing. However, *never* suspend those activities which are certain, or almost certain, to return revenues in excess of the expense they incur. Thus it is unwise to cut expenditures across the board. If any change is made, consideration should be given to increase funding of projects which are strong revenue producing activities. Even here caution must be taken to ensure that such increased funding is increasing net profits.

When cash flow is so low that the institution is unable to cover all its invoices, we have discovered that the best policy to pursue is to pay off all small debts and then send an equal proportion of funds to each major creditor. To ignore these creditors, or some of them, results in reproach to God's cause, to poor credit rating and a loss of credibility in the community. God is dishonored. Business office personnel are bombarded with telephone calls from creditors and often impulsive payments are made to the ignoring of other creditors.

Finally, ever remember that God's people are good and generous. Ever express appreciation for their generous support. Even more, never forget that our wonderful God ultimately supplies all. Love and express deep gratitude to Him.

SUMMARY

1 A strong, effective ministry is the foundation of strong financial support.
2 As soon as possible an institution must seek to be self-sufficient in its operations.
3 College fees should be sufficient to provide all operating costs including—
   a. The salaries of institution staff;
   b. The room and board of the students;
   c. Repairs and maintenance of the buildings;
   d. Utility costs.
4 The cost of student fees should be provided by—
   a. The students' earnest work efforts;
   b. The help of parents if able and willing;
   c. The support of benevolent church members.
5 Solicitation of means should cover a wide range of needs.
   a. Capital items such as buildings, roads, large pieces of equipment, and vehicles;
   b. Financial support for worthy students training for the service of the Lord;

      c. Providing for soul-winning ministry such as literature distribution, outreach and evangelism.
6. The leader and staff of the Stewardship Ministries must be deeply spiritual Christians who are able to minister to the spiritual needs of supporters.
7. It is important for the stewardship division to seek to know where the interest of each donor lies.
8. The stewardship leader needs also to know how to prepare
      a. Wills,
      b. Trusts,
      c. Estate planning, an
      d. How to receive properties, vehicles and equipment.
9. Check carefully before accepting properties. Make sure they are likely to be sold in a reasonable time. Remember that while you own them you pay property tax upon them and must maintain them.
10. Seek also the support of those not of our faith.
11. It is possible to apply for grants from foundations.
12. When in financial difficulties —
      a. Postpone any non-financial generating projects;
      b. *Do not* cut back on funding for activities which will generate returns in excess of expenditure. If possible expend more funding for such projects;
      c. If you do not have funds to pay all creditors, pay the small accounts owed first and then pay whatever percentage you can to all the larger creditors.

Chapter 18

Seminars, Camps and Convocations

IN spite of the intense focus, especially at the commencement of a new institution, to concentrate institutional resources upon the task at hand, as soon as possible there should be an outreach to the Seventh-day Adventist community and to the community at large. Remember that your major financial support will come from dedicated, missionary-minded Seventh-day Adventists. This will provide finance to plan soul-winning outreach to the wider community, and often gifts of needed equipment will also be donated. The most important reason for these meetings, however, is that we have a commission to take the everlasting gospel to the world. Sadly, even among our own church members, there is frequently a pitiful lack of understanding of the great truths which God has entrusted to the Seventh-day Adventist Church.

Let no one forget that the community in which the institute is located is a mission field. The health area is especially designed to open doors for the entry of truth. Later, opportunities will open to present Bible studies, Prophecy seminars, and evangelical crusades. These events should not be infrequent. They provide a wonderful opportunity for people to know and understand and support the ministries.

The success of meetings held for Seventh-day Adventists depends upon the opportunity to advertise widely. The sooner a large mailing list is obtained, the better. Do not limit the institutional outreach to the immediate area where the institution is located. Seek to find support throughout the nation. Send out the institution's best ambassadors as speakers to churches and groups. Some of the most-looked-for speakers are in the fields of health, home schooling, training in soul winning, Bible studies, prophecy, current events and the Bible, end-time events, and simple salvation themes. Send out speaker lists with the themes of the speakers to churches. *Do not* ask for speaking fees but seek either to recover your travelling expenses, or the opportunity for you to call for an offering for your ministry. Give invitations at each meeting to sign up for the mailing list. Then make sure you send regular newsletters from your ministry setting out what you are accomplishing, while also placing the needs of the institution before the readership.

There are other ways to spread the word of upcoming events—public announcements, newspaper articles, announcements in denominational publications, local church meetings, presentations at community centers and senior citizen centers. No matter how few may attend the first meetings, there will be those who will encourage others to come to any future meetings if they have been blessed by the presentations. At each meeting announce the next meeting and encourage attendees to advertise it. Such meetings offer an opportunity to increase the mailing list. Always have quality literature to sell at these meetings together with audios, videos, CDs, and DVDs. If the institution has a health food store, make its goods available; or if it has crops which have been grown in the institute garden, offer them for sale. The success of these continued meetings will depend upon their spiritual quality. Do not compromise the highest standards. Be prepared to travel to make presentations.

It is essential to have a number of annual or even more frequent events on your campus. This allows attendees to be inspired by the dedication of the staff and students, and the ministry being accomplished. Hartland did not take advantage of this on-campus outreach until more than five years after its commencement. This was a serious mistake. We were wonderfully surprised when more than three hundred people attended the first camp meeting. Now it would be unlikely for most to have that number at their first meet-

Seminars, Camps and Convocations

ing, for we had five years to build up our communications. That should not in any way cause a hesitation. Soon many of those in attendance had been so blessed that they were asking for more. Today we have about nine hundred at each camp meeting and our twentieth anniversary camp meeting attracted more than twelve hundred, coming from the six inhabited continents.

Regular meetings provide spiritual rejuvenation and revival to the attendees. We later added an autumn and a spring convocation and eventually also a winter convocation. These now average about five to six hundred attending convocation, the highest being over six hundred and fifty. These are regularly scheduled each year. Whereas the camp meeting extends from Tuesday evening until the following Sunday lunch time, the convocations are held from Friday evening until Sunday lunch time. Our camp meetings offer considerable variety. There are round table discussions each morning where three speakers dialogue on special topics; seminars are offered both in the morning and in the afternoon with normally a choice of three seminars morning and afternoon, presented by different speakers. There are powerful preaching sermons. Sabbath afternoon a sacred musical concert is held. We do not forget the children and youth. We provide special spiritual meetings for all levels, cradle roll to youth. These include special meetings on prophecy, the sanctuary message and righteousness by faith. In every one of these events speakers and teachers are carefully chosen, not to entertain but to provide spiritual inspiration for all of the attendees. Special missionary reports are presented and a number of specific offering appeals are made. Also keep in mind that reaching out to the believers is a rich source for attracting dedicated future staff. Center your offering appeals on special projects. Expense offerings are less attractive to attendees. We explain to the attendees the cost of each camp meeting or convocation and provide an envelope for donations to help cover the costs. From time to time, during the meetings, we announce the progress totals toward the goal.

Other programs should be provided for the community

at large. A variety of forms of health programs, home school seminars, family seminars, youth camps, colporteur seminars, prophecy seminars, salvation principles seminars, "pillars of our faith" seminars, youth health seminars, medical missionary training seminars and foreign language camp meetings all can be conducted on the campus. Set up appointments in churches. The opportunities and the needs are great. The outreach meetings provide a way for the institution to become widely known and its ministry understood.

SUMMARY

1 Reach out early to both Seventh-day Adventist and non-Seventh-day Adventist communities.
2 The primary reason for such outreach is for the salvation of souls.
3 The outreach to Seventh-day Adventists will help in other ways as well. It will provide—
 a. Donations to fund soul-winning activities and other needs.
 b. Equipment donations.
 c. Future dedicated, quality staff.
 d. Volunteer workers from time to time.
4 Advertise speakers and their themes widely by the distribution of invitations.
5 It is best not to ask for speaking fees. However, either suggest that travel expenses be covered or that an offering can be taken to help with expenses.
6 Advertise meetings for Seventh-day Adventists:
 a. In church papers.
 b. Directly to local churches.
7 Advertise meetings for the public through—
 a. Free radio and television community announcements.
 b. Service clubs.
 c. Churches.
 d. Announcements displayed in stores and commercial establishments.

e. Door to door leaflet distribution.
8. Commercial establishments such as banks often offer halls free of charge.
9. Seek to sell to attendees religious and health literature and health foods outside of the Sabbath hours.
10. Arrange for a number of meetings for Seventh-day Adventists and/or the public annually at set times each year.

Chapter 19
The Organizational Chart

WE have been amazed that occasionally we discover a larger self-supporting institution which operates with little delegation of responsibilities. This usually results when one person, because he is the founder of the institution, believes that all decisions must be consistent with his will and ideas. We would suggest that anyone seeking to explore joining a ministry investigate the administrative chart of the organization, looking into the levels and responsibilities of mid-level managers. Inquiries made to staff members will normally provide an initial view of how an institute is operated. Yet one must be judicious in such inquiries as the staff's responses may reflect personal biases for or against the leader. Talk to departmental heads concerning the scope and decision-making freedom that they have.

> The Lord has said, "No one man's mind or judgment is sufficient to exert a controlling influence in any of our institutions." Therefore it is necessary that councils be held, that plans be considered by men of different stamp of character. Then if there are defects, they will be discovered and removed.   *Manuscript Releases*, Vol. 11, 79

At Hartland Institute there are five levels of operational structure—the membership (constituency), the board of directors, the divisional leaders who comprise the administrative committee, the departmental chairman and the staff. Each has very specific responsibilities. There is no individual ownership, for Hartland Institute is a non-profit corporation.

The Constituency

The membership are the trustees and guardians of the institution. The annual membership meeting is the highest authority of the institute. It is the only level of authority which elects itself. Every staff member, as part of his responsibility, is an ex officio member of the constituency of the institution. This provides each staff member with the responsibility to participate in the sacred duty of setting the missionary goals of the institution. Spouses of staff are also encouraged to apply for constituency membership. Every board member is also required to be a constituency member. College students may apply for membership. The membership is open to any individual of good will who is supportive of the goals and philosophies enunciated in the constitution and bylaws, providing that he or she is a faithful Seventh-day Adventist. New members are seated as voting members of the constituency by majority vote of the current constituency. New applications are reviewed at the annual meetings.

The membership is accorded five major responsibilities:

1	It has the solemn responsibility to safeguard the spiritual, doctrinal and operational integrity of the institution.
2	It alone can amend the institute's constitution. Amendments to the constitution require a two-thirds majority vote for passage.
3	It also alone can amend the bylaws, again by a two-thirds vote.
4	The constituency receives the annual reports from the administrative personnel of the institute. This offers opportunity for questioning, advising, and voting upon acceptance of the reports.
5	Reviews the annual auditor's financial report of the Institution.
6	The constituency elects the institute's board members.

At Hartland each constituent serves for a three-year period but can be re-elected indefinitely. It is not wise for the chairman to serve over a long period as he or she is likely to assume a dominant role in the institution. Thus our chairman and vice-chairman by practice serve two-year terms. However, the duration of the term is not defined in Hartland's bylaws. Other institutions may decide to do so. The two-year term does not restrict an individual from serving as chairman again at a later date.

The constituents choose their own chairman and vice-chairman. Three staff members are ex officio members of the board by right of their position and therefore are not elected by the constituency. They are the president, secretary and treasurer of the institute.

Checks and Balances

It is essential for those inaugurating a new institution to exert every effort to establish checks and balances which are designed to secure the integrity and faithfulness of the ministry until the close of human probation. The choice of constituent and board members is of utmost importance because the constituency and the board members hold such crucial decision-making responsibilities. At Hartland, it is usual that more than half of the constituents are staff members and their spouses. They have gone through a most rigorous investigation before they have been appointed as staff.

In evaluating the applications from students, the staff have had the opportunity of very close examination of their dedication and level of commitment to the Lord and are in an informed position to make decisions concerning their suitability to serve on the constituency. The most difficult task is in choosing men and women who are not closely associated with Hartland. It is true, however, that most of those not directly employed by Hartland are people whom many of the staff have come to know very well, in a number of capacities. Most have frequently attended camp meetings, convocations and other events which are planned at or by Hartland Institute. Most are regular donors to Hartland. Some are the parents of students studying at Hartland. Others are former staff members. However, where there is any significant lack of knowledge of the qualities of the applicant, special inquiry takes place.

Each applicant is required to fill out a formal application providing information concerning background, beliefs and experience and understanding of the philosophy of Hartland Institute. On occasions we have received applications from those whom we do not know. Should they not appear at a subsequent constituency meeting no action is taken. It is important for new applicants to be present at the constituency meeting so that any questions concerning their eligibility and suitability to serve in such an important capacity can be reviewed by questioning and dialogue.

The membership of Hartland is in excess of one hundred constituents.

The Board of Directors

Board members are elected to a three-year term. Approximately one-third of the seventeen elected board members come up for reelection each year. If there is a resignation or death of a board member before the expiration of that board member's term, the replacement, chosen by the board, serves out the remaining portion of the previous board member's term before facing reelection again. The reason that we have staggered elections for board members is to ensure the major continuity of the institution and to avoid the very unlikely possibility of a hostile take-over which could lead to an alteration in the ideals and direction of the institution.

The board of directors meets regularly twice a year, though an extraordinary board meeting may be called at any time. Such an extraordinary Board meeting may meet at Hartland or may transact its business by a telephone conference or, on smaller matters, by email vote. The board votes its own chairman and vice-chairman. Both are appointed for a one year term. It has been the practice at Hartland Institute for chairman and vice-chairman to serve a two-year term before new leadership is chosen. Once again there is reason for this. It is believed by Hartland personnel that a chairperson who serves overlong becomes too dominant in the decision- making affairs of the institution, rather than permitting those decisions to come from a wide spectrum of thinking. On occasions choices for chairmanship have been made of those who have already served in the past but have spent at least two years out of office between the first and second or any future terms.

The board is responsible for voting all the major institution-wide decisions. Generally speaking these major decisions come as recommendations from the administrative committee. However, board members themselves may also introduce major new initiatives. The board decisions are normally final and the administrative committee is entrusted with the responsibility of implementing them. If on rare occasions the administration finds that some aspects of the project appear to lack feasibility when attempt is made to implement it, the administrative committee can have recourse again to the board for approval of a suggested modification of the original decision.

The board of directors appoints the administrators of the institution annually. At present there are eight administrators who are board-appointed. At Hartland these are the president, treasurer, dean of the college, director of the Wellness Center, director of Hartland Publications, director of World Missions, director of the Stewardship Ministries, and director of Plant Services. The board also elects the officers of the institute—the president, the secretary and the treasurer. Normally, the president and treasurer of the corporation are those who serve as president and treasurer of the institution. The secretary of the organization has the responsibility to be secretary to the Board, to the Administrative Committee, and for executing corporate and legal matters on behalf of the Corporation, Board and Administrative Committee.

The board of directors receives reports at its biannual meetings from all the administrators although, as the second board meeting of the year is held after the constituency meeting, the constituency members review and vote the annual reports while the board discusses any matter which arises out of the reports, or from discussion of the reports by the members.

The Administrative Committee

The Administrative Committee consists of all the divisional leaders. The committee is scheduled to meet every two weeks and is chaired in rotation among the administrators. Each serves for a three-month period as chairman, each administrator serving in rotation. This practice has taken place for many years, established upon the principle that no single individual in the institution should have the authority to dominate the decision making of the institution.

The Administrative Committee is entrusted with the responsibility of supplementing all board-voted actions. It, as a general rule, does not decide individual cases but rather addresses institution-wide matters and matters which affect more than one division. Even many of the latter decisions are decided by dialogue of the respective leaders.

The Administrative Committee determines the spiritual and doctrinal suitability of any staff applicant who has applied for a position in the institution.

The Administrative Committee is responsible to prepare the annual proposed budget for the Spring Board Meeting.

Standing Committees

The larger divisions have standing committees. The college has the largest number of standing committees. They include academic affairs, citizenship, curriculum, student finance and admissions committees. The Wellness Center has the general staff, interdisciplinary care plan and medical review committees. From time to time the board, the administrative committee and the individual divisions may appoint ad hoc committees.

Divisional leaders are responsible for strict budget control of expenditures in their divisions, and for all other fiscal decisions.

Departmental heads

Within each division there are department supervisors. Each of the college academic departments has a chairperson. The four chairpersons respectively supervise the Bible, Education, Health and Publishing departments. The Wellness center has departmental leaders in the Business Office, the Dietary Department, Therapy, Hydro-Massage and Exercise, and Medical. The Plant Services Division has the following departments: New Construction, Maintenance, Automotive Service, Grounds maintenance and Agriculture. The Stewardship Ministries Division Departments are:

Sustaining Gifts;
Special Gifts;
Estate Planning:
 a) wills,
 b) trusts,
 c) bequests;
Public Relations:
 a) Hartland Ministry Report,
 b) Donor relations;
Sales of Gifts in Kind:
 a) property,
 b) cars/vehicles,
 c) collectibles/antiques.

World Missions departments are Bible Conference and Evangelism. Hartland Publications comprises Customer Service, Shipping and Receiving, Book Publication–New and Reprints, Accounts Payable and Receivable, and the Media Center.

The Staff

Some staff members, of course, have no specific leadership roles but they may serve on standing committees. Also, from time to time, staff members are appointed to ad hoc committees. We have found at Hartland that the careful division of responsibilities is essential for the checks and balances necessary to make sure that no individual or small group controls the activities and direction of the institution. Significantly, Hartland Institute is so organized that even the most junior staff member has a say at the top level of organization, management and decision-making as a member of the constituency of the institution. These features of organization have been carefully planned and the staff believes that the Lord has led. We know of no other self-supporting institution which is so carefully organized. In fact, few self-supporting institutions have a constituency. Therefore the board members choose themselves, a practice that can result in self-serving consequences.

The Goals

It has been the desire of the architects of Hartland Institute that every opportunity will be given to maintain the spiritual and ministry goals upon which it was founded, and to increase the effectiveness of the ministry through the function of all levels of organization. We seek to make sure that the voice of God can be heard and followed by faithful people associated with the institution. There is a jealous guarding of the sacred trust that God has placed in our care, for we realize that Satan has found a way to derail every God-established institution in the history of the world, beginning with the Eden school. Many ministries start up with impeccable Biblical principles but as the years pass and new leaders, staff and board members are appointed, step by tragic step these lead those institutions into apostasy.

Qualification for Service

It is rare for anyone to be chosen as a board member who has not had a long-standing association with Hartland Institute. Of course, at the beginning that was not possible. However, in the case of the establishment of Hartland Institute, before the first official board was established, an interim board was elected which served for almost a year before it was seen that sufficient information was available so that an official board could be elected. Of course, a number of those who had been members of the interim board were also chosen to serve on the original board. With over twenty years of experience now, all those who are elected to the Board have been known for many years to the staff and administration of Hartland Institute. They have proven their support and shown their consistency with the goals, purposes and mission of the institute, and fidelity to Bible truth.

There are many qualifications which are important for members of both the constituency and board to evidence. First, all must be dedicated to the hastening of the return of Jesus Christ. All must be faithful Seventh-day Adventists who have not been swayed by the New Theology apostasy or the multitudinous winds of doctrine which have been thrust at the church. They have to understand that our first loyalty is to God and that no edict of man will influence them away from a plain "Thus saith the Lord." However they will not be among those who believe the Seventh-day Adventist Church is Babylon. They will include men and women who believe that while the structure of the church will be swept away ("storm and tempest would sweep away the structure" (*Selected Messages*, Book. 1, 205), they understand that it will be the ultimate and complete sifting and shaking which will cleanse God's church (see *Last Day Events*, 173) preparatory to the reception of the latter rain, the completion of the gospel commission and the Second Coming of Jesus.

> Under the showers of the latter rain the inventions of man, the human machinery, will at times be swept away, the boundary of man's authority will be as broken reeds, and the Holy Spirit will speak through the living, human agent, with convincing power.
> *Selected Messages*, Book. 2, 58, 59

> . . . but now he hath promised saying, Yet once more I shake not the earth only, but also heaven. And this word, yet once more, signifieth the removing of those things that are shaken, as of things that are made, that those things which cannot be shaken may remain.
> Hebrews 12:26, 27

> We are in the shaking time, the time when everything that can be shaken will be shaken. *Testimonies*, vol. 6, 332

Those who serve with Hartland Institute are people who provide evidence that they know the precious truths of God's Word and understand the educational, health, publishing and ministry principles which the Bible and Spirit of Prophecy have provided for us. They will be people who themselves are actively engaged in witnessing the truth to others. Too much is at stake to make careless decisions in the choice of people for these positions. While we pray earnestly for God to protect His institution, we realize that we are expected to make sure that His institution will not be compromised by unfaithful or ill-informed people. It is Hartland's goal to be a model which others seeking to establish an institution can look to as a pattern that can safely guide them. That is the reason that the Hartland model has been used in this chapter.

SUMMARY

1 Careful attention must be given to the organizational structure of an institution.
2 We believe large institutions require a constituency, board, administration and staff.
3 The role of the constituency:
   a. Hasten the coming of Jesus.
   b. Safeguard the spiritual, doctrinal and organizational integrity of the institution.
   c. Meet at least once a year to examine reports from the Administration.
   d. Make the major directional decisions for the institution.
   e. Amend the constitution if desirable. Such amendments require at least a two-thirds majority.
   f. Amend the by-laws, requiring at least a two-thirds majority.
   g. Elect board members.
   h. Review the annual auditor's report of the institutes' financial operations.
4 Suggested composition of the Constituency:
   a. Board Members,
   b. Administrators,
   c. All staff,
   d. Students, if there is a college-level school,
   e. Other faithful supporters of the institution.

5 The role of the Board of Directors:
a. Hasten the coming of Jesus.
    b. Safeguard the integrity of the spiritual and doctrinal emphasis of the institution.
    c. Maintain the adherence of the institute to divine counsel.
    d. Appoint administrators to lead the institute and each division.
    e. Appoint ad hoc and standing committees.
    f. Approve the annual budget.
    g. Review the institute master plan.
    h. Approve major construction and development.

6 The role of Administrators:
    a. Hasten the coming of Jesus.
    b. Safeguard the spiritual and doctrinal emphasis of the institution.
    c. Be responsible for the administration of the institute.
    d. Address decisions dealing with institution-wide issues.
    e. Review staff applicants for spiritual, lifestyle, doctrinal and financial suitability prior to a decision by the divisional leader.
    f. Operate the institution with financial soundness.
    g. Prepare the proposed annual budget for the board.
    h. Prepare biannual reports for the constituency and board.

7 Division Leaders:
    a. Hasten the coming of Jesus.
    b. Lead the division within the principles of divine counsel.
    c. Run the day by day operations of the division to which they have oversight.
    d. Appoint staff after a favorable review of their suitability, spirituality, life-style and doctrinal integrity by the Administrative Committee.
    e. Be responsible for all fiscal decisions in their divisions and for responsible budget control for their division.

Chapter 20

Governance in Self-Supporting Work

THERE is little specific counsel from the Lord concerning the form of governance to be employed in self-supporting institutions. However, we do have plain counsel to the Seventh-day Adventist Church's denominational leaders. These principles must be taken and applied also in the governance of a lay or self-supporting ministry. The founders of the Seventh-day Adventist Church came from various church organizations with various forms of governance. As almost all pioneer Seventh-day Adventists came from the Protestant heritage, it was easy to reject the papal hierarchical form of church governance where one man, the leader of the organization, assumes ultimate authority in the organization. Seventh-day Adventists rejected the Episcopal form of church governance as practiced in the Anglican and the Episcopal Churches. In such governance the bishops assume an authority in their dioceses that has major unilateral decision-making power within the diocese. The Bishops have untoward authority over the priests who serve in the diocese.

Some early Seventh-day Adventists advocated and practiced a congregational form of church governance in which each individual congregation had full directional and decision making authority. Such a form of governance is well known among Congregationalists and Baptists. However, God did not choose the congregational form of church governance for His church. Rather God presented His perfect pattern of representative governance in which responsibility and authority is invested in the local churches (See Colin and

Russell Standish, *Organizational Structure and Apostasy*). Local churches have the responsibility to accept new members into the worldwide Seventh-day Adventist Church and also the responsibility to censure or disfellowship members who are, for one reason or another, misrepresenting the Seventh-day Adventist faith in matters of doctrine or in patterns of lifestyle and practice. Representatives from each church in the Conference participating also share heavy responsibility in guiding the work of the Conference and participating in the election of Conference officials. The delegates representing the constituent churches of the Conference have great sacred authority. They have the authority to vote to amend the constitution and by-laws of the Conference and set the agenda for the Conference President and the Conference Executive Committee.

At the Union level, the constituent Conferences set the agenda, choose the leadership, and are authorized to amend the Union constitution and by-laws. Representative laypeople also are appointed along with church workers as delegates to the Union Constituency. At the General Conference level, it is the Unions which have similar responsibilities for the General Conference. Laity are elected also to the General Conference Constituency now held every five years. The representative form of governance given to our church by God does not allow for dictatorship from above. Ultimately, the responsibility resides largely with the local church. This is the divine plan which was set before God's church. Sister White was greatly perturbed by the fact that so many leaders had assumed kingly power within a few decades of the establishment of the General Conference. Therefore she wrote passionately against kingly power and "rule or ruin governance." She warned that if the cords were tightened, the laity would rise up and exercise their freedom in Christ.

> If the cords are drawn much tighter, if the rules are made much finer, if men continue to bind their fellow-laborers closer and closer to the commandments of men, many will be stirred by the Spirit of God to break every shackle, and

assert their liberty in Christ Jesus.
Review and Herald, July 23, 1895

Church members who have seen the light and been convicted, but who have trusted the salvation of their souls to the minister, will learn in the day of God that no other soul can pay the ransom for their transgression. A terrible cry will be raised, "I am lost, eternally lost." Men will feel as though they could rend in pieces the ministers who have preached falsehoods and condemned the truth.
Last Day Events, 247

God has not set any kingly power in the Seventh-day Adventist Church to control the whole body or to control any branch of the work. He has not provided that the burden of leadership shall rest upon a few men. Responsibilities are distributed among a large number of competent men.
Testimonies, Vol. 8, 236

God will not vindicate any device whereby man shall in the slightest degree rule or oppress his fellowman. As soon as a man begins to make an iron rule for other men, he dishonors God and imperils his own soul and the souls of his brethren.
Ibid., Vol. 7, 181

Men have taken unfair advantage of those whom they supposed to be under their jurisdiction. They were determined to bring the individuals to their terms; they would rule or ruin.
Last Day Events, 49

But the rule-or-ruin system is too often seen in our institutions. This spirit is cherished and revealed in some in responsible positions, and because of this, God cannot do the work He desires to do through them.
Testimonies to Ministers, 280

Let us apply the same plan of God to self-supporting institutions. It has been our observation that many self-supporting leaders, some of whom are quite critical of denominational leaders who assume the role of a virtual dictator, are themselves seeking dictatorial power. This situation is especially true when an institution has been established primarily by one person. Such individuals in many cases have a tendency to assume the role of an owner of a business. If such takes place he is certain to treat his colleagues as employees rather than associates in the work of God. This is one reason why self-supporting institutions often have a very rapid turnover of personnel. However, it would be too simplistic to say that this was the only reason for the staff turnover. There are other causes. Obviously the usual sacrificial stipends which are provided for self-supporting workers are another contributing factor. It is also a fact, generally speaking, that self-supporting workers are very deeply convicted, and sometimes convictions of one do not coincide with the convictions of the major portion of the workers. This leads also to staff attrition.

Christ has provided the divine plan for leaders. They are to be servant-leaders.

> But Jesus called them unto him, and said, Ye know that the princes of the Gentiles exercise dominion over them, and they that are great exercise authority upon them. But it shall not be so among you: but whosoever will be great among you, let him be your minister; and whosoever will be chief among you, let him be your servant: even as the Son of man came not to be ministered unto, but to minister, and to give his life a ransom for many.
> Matthew 20:25–28

> But be not ye called Rabbi: for one is your Master, even Christ and all ye are brethren.   Matthew 23:8

> The elders which are among you I exhort, who am also an elder, and a witness of the sufferings of Christ, and also a partaker of the glory that shall be revealed: feed the flock of God which is among you, taking the oversight thereof, not by constraint, but willingly; not for filthy lucre, but of a ready mind; Neither as being lords over God's heritage, but being ensamples to the flock. And when the chief Shepherd shall appear, ye shall receive a crown of glory that fadeth not away.   1 Peter 5:1–4

This is the perfect leadership model of which both Moses and Paul were taught by God.

Governance in Self-Supporting Work

> In the military schools of Egypt, Moses was taught the law of force, and so strong a hold did this teaching have upon his character that it required forty years of quiet and communion with God and nature to fit him for the leadership of Israel by the law of love. The same lesson Paul had to learn. — *Education*, 65

These are the principles which every godly leader must learn.

Using the divine model of the representative form of governance, no matter how involved a foundational leader in an institution may be, it is his duty to share the responsibility of leadership with others. This sharing is indispensable to achieving success. If true success is to be achieved in self-supporting institutions, lay organizations and all of God's institutions, true participatory involvement must be provided. This requires much more than choosing support leaders whose only real responsibility is to rubber stamp the concepts of the leader. Only weak personnel will be prepared to continue in such a situation. The institution will be no stronger, and will move no further than the length and breath of the ideas of one man or woman under such governance.

Autocratic leadership leads to the loss of good personnel, men and women essential to the broadening and the strengthening of the organization. Frequently there is a head-on collision between the leader and his capable subordinate. This usually results in an individual being forced out of the institution or dismissed on the grounds of insubordination. No lay constituency or board can afford to do nothing in such circumstances. The institution Board and its Constituency must accept the responsibility of determining the reasons why staff members are leaving and evaluate the frequency of such departures. The role of the institutional leader and the Administrative Committee in these departures must be evaluated.

It must ever be remembered that the Holy Spirit can guide every dedicated member of staff regardless of the post he or she holds.

The American work force is very mobile. The worker

averages only a little more than four years in one position. Various factors can change that. When there is a downturn in the economy, staff are less likely to resign, for alternate work opportunities are limited. In normal times the ambitious seek upward mobility so are more likely to change positions and work places. Recently it was reported on the Washington, D.C. news station, WTOP, that those joining the work force now were predicted to change jobs twelve times during their work-life.

In self-supporting work the turnover is usually high. The average turnover is not infrequently less than four years. If this be the case, it is cause for concern. It is expensive to have frequent changes in personnel. Each time a worker departs much experience is lost. A new staff member may take much training if he accepts an advanced position. Further, properly qualified replacements for such roles are rarely easy to find. It is not always easy to discover the genuine reason why staff leave. Leaving staff will not always provide the most important reason. All existing institutions should be supportive of the establishment of new ministries. There should be a rapidly increasing number of lay personnel who have learned much from the experience of serving in an established institution. It is one of the duties of self-supporting ministries to be training grounds for employed workers. Now, if any one of those workers believes that he or she has been called to apply that experience in a new field, he or she should leave with the blessing of the remainder of the staff.

If staff members are alert, they will sometimes hear comments, not always complimentary, concerning the governance style of the leader. It is wise to ignore these comments unless the hearer has noticed the same negative characteristic. It takes courage to seek to address the issue in Christian concern with one's leader. If a worker's advice is correct, and is accepted, he or she has added much to the success of God's work. If the suggestion is not accepted, the worker may still be assured of the approbation of God. Leaders should be encouraged to provide a participatory form of governance and to provide a framework of administrative organization which will ensure that the leader does not take unilateral power, authority and decision making. If a leader is bent on dictatorial leadership and all suggested corrective measures fail, the leader should be removed or reassigned by placing him in a less controlling position. Usually it is necessary to release him from all his responsibilities at the institute. This is an action which often causes much anguish, especially when he has been central to the organization. However, it may be the only recourse left to a wise board of directors if the institute's primary goals and vision are to be met.

Not long ago a leader of a self-supporting institution was counseled by a much older man who had been his teacher at college. This leader had developed serious problems with his faulted over-control of his staff. This leadership style had already led to a number of acrimonious splits in the organization. The wise counselor urged the leader to reform his overbearing and often acrimonious style of leadership. Unfortunately the response of the leader was "This is *my* show and I intend to keep it that way." Such leadership is not of God.

A good leader is a good delegator. He will realize that, if the staff has been wisely chosen, every one will know much more than he does about some important facet of the work of the institution. The leader must be so assured of the leading of God in his life that he will never feel threatened by the superior knowledge and ability of another in one or more areas of the institution. He will vigorously seek talented men and women to enhance greatly his contribution to the thrust of God's work in the institution. It is a weak leader who deliberately chooses fellow workers whose level of skills is such that they do not threaten his leadership ego. The leader should not only seek the very best and talented staff, but seek to find someone to be his ultimate successor.

SUMMARY

1. God has chosen the representative form of governance for His church.
   a. No leader under God will use force.
   b. No leader can rightfully choose dictatorial leadership models.
   c. God's leaders are servant-leaders.
   d. The true governance is that of participation by all.
   e. Delegation is key to a successful organization.
   f. Delegation does not equate with abdication of the leader's responsibilities.
   g. There will, however, be no kingly power exercised.
2. Staff resignations.
   a. Try to discover the reasons for resignation of staff.
   b. Remember that you will not always receive the primary reason without persistent, gentle investigation.
   c. If the average stay of staff is short (less than four years is a good guide), analyze the reasons.
   d. It could be poor initial selection of a staff member or unfulfilled expectations in the minds of the resigning staff member.

Chapter 21
The Choice of Staff

THE choice of staff is the most important responsibility which the administration of an institution undertakes. So careful is the administrative committee at Hartland to do all in its power to investigate staff members, that no one is appointed to an administrative position when first entering service at Hartland. Most administrators have worked for some time at Hartland before being chosen to serve in an administrative role.

If one has been chosen as a possible leader of a division, he or she will first be appointed by the Administrative Committee as an *acting* divisional leader. Being chosen as an acting leader does not automatically ensure that the candidate will be recommended to the board to be confirmed as a divisional leader. The minimum time which an acting leader serves in that capacity, whether relatively new or having served for many years at Hartland, will be six months. Usually the acting divisional leader has held the acting post considerably longer than six months. The acting status has been held as long as two years, before a final decision has been made. Hartland's board alone can appoint an administrator to a permanent position.

It is the goal of the administration, and especially the president, to seek to counsel and help all staff in areas where growth is necessary or where improvement needs to be made. No matter what role is to be played, the investigation is always rigorous and careful, for we know that these staff members have the responsibility to act as models to the students and to provide a pattern of life from which the students can confidently learn.

We recognize that no matter the role in which a staff member serves, he still has a great influence for good or evil, truth or error upon the students. Thus in choosing leaders in practical areas such as janitorial duties, the farm, or plant service, the review is just as rigorous as in the selection of the classroom teachers. Administrators bear in mind that at Hartland all students undertake sixteen hours of vocational training a week under the supervision of a wide range of staff personnel, especially in the practical areas. Therefore it is essential that all staff be able to provide sound, valuable Christian counsel to the students and to help them to understand some of the great truths that God has entrusted to us. Obviously the student can develop a close relationship with his vocational supervisor, and in a less formal setting will often spend more time, and therefore ask more questions, or discuss more issues with his work supervisor than with the academic teacher. Those considerations underlie the reason why the choice of staff to any position is critical.

It is surprising to some that self-supporting work requires not only a more spiritual staff than any other form of Christian service, but also more talented and effective workers. One of the most common mistakes of self-supporting institutions is to accept eagerly all volunteers who may offer their service. This is especially true in the formative years of the organization. Such an approach can bring only weakness and anguish to the institution. Many who seek to attach themselves to a self-supporting institution are wholly unacceptable. The main areas of unsuitability include:

1   Those who are not able to hold down a regular job either for lack of skills or lack of productivity.
2   Those who live essentially a nomadic life and who will stay for a very short period of time before moving on.
3   Those who have a history of a disagreeable personality and who will almost certainly bring a level of negativism into the institution.
4   Those who have unstable temperaments and personalities.

The Choice of Staff

5   Those who are emotionally unstable and who imagine that a change in environment will make a dramatic improvement to their emotional health.
6   Those who, while exhibiting deep spirituality, expect to be able to spend large blocks of time each day in study of spiritual material, ignoring the great needs of productive labor in self-supporting institutions. They forget the divine counsel that there is a time for everything.

> To every thing there is a season, and a time to every purpose under the heaven. Ecclesiastes 3:1

7   Those who have serious physical ailments.
8   Those who have accepted winds of doctrine, believing that in a self-supporting institution they will find a fruitful field for sharing these doctrines.

It is better, far better, to leave an important position unfilled than to appoint the wrong person. It is much less painful to reject an applicant than to later have to release him from service. At Hartland Institute, the administration has waited up to seven years to make an appointment rather than appoint someone who would be ineffective. For example, this policy was followed in such an important role as the head of the Stewardship Ministries Division. The divisional leaders were given the responsibility to carry out this role for seven years until they were able to find a qualified person to fulfill the responsibility. In our initial start up we waited three years for a suitable farm manager, critical though this role was to our ministry. Others did their best in training the first students in gardening until a qualified man was available.

Usually, of course, the wait will not be a matter of years. Hasty decisions all too frequently end with long-term headaches. It is not fair to the applicant any more than to the institution to undertake only a superficial review of the applicant's qualifications. Over the years, Hartland has strengthened its application and interview process. Colin at first started to implement such a program when he was President of Columbia Union College in Maryland; however, we have a much more effective system today. This is not to suggest that even with the very best application instrument and the best interview process, mistakes are not made. But it is our responsibility to minimize the likelihood of such a result.

There have been occasions when we have asked the applicant to spend time studying the pillar truths of the Seventh-day Adventist message thoroughly before making a reapplication. This happens only if the committee believes the applicant has quality skills important to the Institute's needs. Others are asked to come as volunteers for periods as long as three months so that both the applicant and the administrators can evaluate whether the individual and the institute are certain that God is calling each one.

Our application forms are extensive. Only when we receive a fully completed application form is there a review by all the administrators. At a subsequent Administrative Committee meeting the application is reviewed, every division leader being given the opportunity to express an interest in the applicant. If there is no interest or need by any of the administrators, the application is rejected. If one or more division leader(s) be interested in hiring the applicant, then it is regular practice to invite the applicant for a personal interview, preferably with spouse and children. Self-supporting work employs a family. That must always be kept in mind. Families, generally speaking, cost more to the institution, but our considerations go much deeper than that. Even if a spouse does not apply for a position, he or she must also be adjudged to be compatible with the goals of the institution. The character and influence of the children is essential information. We have had to reject applications from excellent prospects because of a serious problem with their children.

While the final decision to employ—or not to employ—an applicant resides with the division leader and staff who has invited the applicant; nevertheless, all administrators, as far as possible, are present at the on-site interview. Their questions are focused upon spiritual, doctrinal and life-style issues. If these issues, together with financial considerations, are a good match, the Administrator is free to appoint the staff member. There is a review of the new staff member three months after commencing service at the institute. Further, the applicant and his family also have the opportunity to ask questions of the administrators. It is only after such an interview that a decision is made as to the suitability of the applicant. Of course, if invited to join the staff, the applicant also has to be assured that he/she is being led to Hartland.

To some, the administration's care in appointing new members to the staff may be judged to be too strict, but it has worked very well for Hartland, and has paid dividends in greatly reducing the number of disappointed workers and the number of administrative staff difficulties. Hartland Administrators believe that God has called the Institute to a high and holy mission, and as such the greatest care must be exercised to assure that the mission is undertaken in holiness and at the highest level of competence. Nothing less would honor our God.

SUMMARY

1 Staff applicants must be thoroughly reviewed before acceptance.
2 Once a staff member is accepted there should be a review process three to six months after taking up responsibilities.
3 It is wise to appoint a new administrator to an acting position until proven capable of leading the division.
4 All staff must be capable of providing wise counsel to students.
5 Avoid appointing those who—
   a. are incapable of holding down a job in the outside world.
   b. have a history of a nomadic life-style.
   c. are disagreeable.
   d. have erratic temperaments and personalities.
   e. are emotionally unstable.
   f. expect time from their work schedule to do their spiritual study.
   g. have serious physical ailments.

    h. have accepted winds of doctrine.
    i. are not grounded in Bible truth
6. Make no rush appointment. Wait, if necessary, for the right person for the responsibility.
7. Thoroughly check the spiritual and doctrinal integrity of the applicant.
8. It is worth the cost of interviewing the whole family before deciding the choice of an applicant.
9. Remember that the ministry is only as effective as the quality of the staff.

Chapter 22

The Applicant Interview

THE interview for new staff applications at Hartland Institute follows a very predictable line of questioning. It begins with the spiritual life of the applicant. Some of the questions which are asked include:

1   Have you read the Bible through?
2   What Spirit of Prophecy books have you read cover to cover?
3   Do you have daily private devotions?
4   Married applicants are asked "Do you have morning and evening family worship?"
5   Inquiry is made of married applicants as to the strength of their marriage.
6   As you bring a family to the institution, the children, if any, should be evaluated as to their likely influence on the campus.
7   If there has been a divorce or more than one divorce, then it is important to know whether there have been Biblical grounds for remarriage, should the divorcee be remarried.
8   Church affiliation is explored. No one is excluded from service if he or she has been disfellowshipped on non-Biblical grounds (though all Hartland staff hold local church membership).
9   Questions concerning positions of service held in church are asked.
10   Inquiries are made concerning involvement in outreach ministries.
11   The applicant is questioned concerning his or her reasons

for seeking to be part of Hartland's ministry.

Then follows a series of questions dealing with doctrinal beliefs. The applicant is asked straightforward questions focused upon the pillars of our faith. These include such questions as:

1. What transpired in 1844?
2. Explain the salient features of the sanctuary message.
3. What is Christ, as our High Priest, accomplishing for His people today?
4. The applicant's understanding of the Three Angels' Messages.
5. Other key doctrines are discussed.

We also seek to discover whether the applicant espouses the elements of the New Theology errors and winds of doctrine. Questions are asked concerning such matters as:

1. Christ's human nature.
2. The non-eternal existence of Christ.
3. The observance of the Old Testament feast days.
4. The focus on the Hebrew word for God.
5. The Wednesday crucifixion.
6. The identification of Satan as the second beast of Reveltion 13.
7. The discounting of the dates 538 and 1798.

There is yet another line of questioning. This details whether the candidates for staff positions are supportive of the major inspired standards which we uphold. These include:

1. Sabbath-keeping.
2. Health Reform.
3. Recreation standards.
4. Social relations for both staff and students.
5. Dress reform.
6. Tithing.

It is ever uppermost in the minds of the Administrative

Committee that every staff member, aside from other responsibility, is a role model for our students.

Only after the Administrative Committee is satisfied that the applicant is a person of spiritual fidelity, that the Administrative Committee addresses the skills of the applicant—training, experience and suitability for a particular role. It is also helpful to seek to understand the applicant's interest and skill in training young people who will be assigned to him or her in work experience. We believe that such a thorough investigation is essential not only for the onward integrity of the institution, but that it is only fair that the applicant know Hartland's standards, to be able to decide whether he or she shares those principles. It is after this in depth interview that the Administrative Committee members discuss the applicant's qualifications, but not at this point to decide whether to offer employment. The Administrative Committee has veto only in four areas—spirituality, doctrinal integrity, compatibility with God-given standards, and finances.

Normally, the finances have already been reviewed before the applicant is brought for interview. The Administrative Committee requires that the division of Hartland Institute seeking to employ the new staff member have the necessary resources. Normally, if the application is to replace a staff member, there are few questions pertaining to this matter unless there has been a downward turn in the economic health of that division. Every division leader has the right to make the decision whether the individual interviewed has the skills necessary to fit the available vacancy. If more than one division is interested in the applicant, it is left to those division leaders to negotiate the matter of which division is most in need of this applicant or, alternatively, if it is possible to share the applicant on a half-time basis. Such decisions are normally worked out amicably and quickly. Sometimes the applicant expresses a preference for the division in which he or she desires to serve.

After three months' probation in the new role, the staff member's performance is reviewed by the division leader. This interview determines whether the new worker is confirmed in the position, or whether a further three months' probation is needed after the administrator has indicated weaknesses to be addressed. The second review could, but rarely does, lead to the ending of the individual's service at Hartland.

Before the applicant is called for an interview there are a number of preliminary checks which are made.

1. Obviously we are interested in the position for which the applicant has applied. Every now and again we receive an application which says something to the effect "Wherever needed." Rarely do we accept such an applicant. Hartland has very specific needs which require people with specific training, talent and experience.
2. We check the applicant's work history. A series of short-term service at a significant number of different places is a red flag to us, for the chances are that such a person will last only a short time at Hartland. Because of the expenses and the disruption which frequent staff changes bring, rarely is such a person considered seriously.
3. We check references carefully.

This may all seem to be far beyond the normal investigations for the selection of staff. Some might be asking how we ever find staff while upholding such high expectations. However, this is the secret of the quality of the staff who serve at Hartland Institute. We have discovered that the more carefully we screen applicants before their employment, the greater the contribution made by new staff.

Yet it is not always easy to attract the finest staff, especially in a place like Hartland where we need well trained staff while offering only sacrificial stipends. Hartland employs many specialists. In the various divisions such are essential to the overall success of the Institution. We list some of these:

1. Wellness Center:
   a. Director
   b. Physicians
   c. Nurses

The Applicant Interview

    d. Hydrotherapists
    e. Health educators
    f. Massage and exercise specialists
    g. Nutritionists/dieticians/food service specialists

2 Hartland Publications, which is staffed by:
    a. Director
    b. Authors
    c. Editors
    d. Proof readers
    e. Business people
    f. Warehousemen
    g. Media center specialists
    h. Customer service specialists

3 Hartland College:
    a. Dean
    b. Educators
    c. Bible and Evangelistic Teachers
    d. Health Educators
    e. Publication specialists
    f. Outreach directors
    g. Admissions Director
    h. Registrar

4 Stewardship Ministries:
    a. Director
    b. Trust Services specialists
    c. Fund raising specialists
    d. Periodicals editor

5 World Missions:
    a. Director
    b. Camp and convocation organizer
    c. Weekend Bible Conference organizer
    d. Evangelistic outreach planner
    e. Travel specialist

6 General Administrative Services:
    a. Administrators
    b. Treasurer
    c. Bookkeepers
    d. Word processors

    e. Receptionists
7 Plant Services:
    a. Agriculture
    b. Construction
    c. Maintenance
    d. Grounds care
    e. Auto mechanics
    f. Janitorial services

Colin has discovered that any institution which will follow God's plan may be tested, but will ultimately be blessed with faithful staff members.

SUMMARY

1 Spiritual Issues:
    a. When interviewing prospective staff, seek first to understand the level of spiritual commitment.
    b. Then evaluate the spiritual development of the children if there be any.
    c. Seek to establish the family's commitment to private and family worship.
    d. Does applicant have a deep commitment to present truth?
    e. Does he or she have a record of Christian service in the church and community?
    f. Is the applicant attracted to speculative theology and winds of doctrine?
    g. Is the family bond strong in the Lord?
2 Reform Issues:
    a. Sabbath reform
    b. Health reform
    c. Recreational reform
    d. Dress reform
    e. Social relations reform
3 Suitability for the position:
    a. Educational background
    b. Experience background
    c. Efficiency and work ethic

d. Versatility
   e. Evidence of a cooperative team person
   f. Evidence of leadership qualities and training capabilities
4 New Staff:
   a. Assign someone to orient new staff members to their new roles.
   b. Be available to answer their questions.
   c. Evaluate new staff after about three months, in a helpful and supportive atmosphere.
   d. Let staff know you appreciate their efforts.

Chapter 23

In-Service Training of Institutional Personnel

NO MATTER how well prepared a new staff member may be for the responsibilities which he or she has undertaken at the institution, there is an ongoing need for further in-service training. Because the cost of training through seminars, conferences and conventions can be formidable, it is important to design in-service training which can be accomplished in the institution itself, led by the trained, experienced personnel already on the staff. In an institution such as Hartland, worship, chapel exercises, prayer meetings and vespers services offer very important regularly-scheduled services which are critical to the onward spiritual, moral and doctrinal development of all the staff. It is therefore important that attendance at all or most of these meetings be required of staff members. Such meetings are also essential for the achievement of unity and spiritual harmony on key topics of the great pillars of our faith. These should be frequently brought before staff members. The belief in, and the following of divine counsel should not be taken for granted. There is always room for growth and the acquirement of a deeper understanding for all staff members. So important are these required services that they should be factored into the forty hours per week of ministry expected of every staff member.

There is also the need for regular staff meetings. Staff meetings provide a splendid opportunity to keep the staff well informed upon the developments which the administration is planning, the decisions taken at board and administrative meetings, and to provide a time to canvass new ideas with the staff. Hartland staff meetings are not only a time for administration to share its visions and ideas and actions, but it is also an opportunity for staff members to provide their own input. Therefore staff should have the opportunity to place their own items on the agenda. However, a staff meeting is not a forum to publicize personal grievances nor to agitate private agendas. Those matters should be taken up in a more appropriate forum, with individual administrators or with the Administrative Committee; or, if of sufficient import, with the board of directors.

Beside general staff meetings there should be divisional or departmental meetings where leaders at this level spend time with their staff members. In some areas especially, there should be committees which have decision-making responsibilities. For example, Hartland College has an Academic Affairs Committee of which the entire college staff are members. There are also Curriculum, Citizenship, Finance, and Admissions Committees which have decision-making authority. In no manner should leaders believe that they can operate effectively without wide consultation with fellow staff members. A leader is to serve and not to rule. However, leaders are obligated to motivate and offer new ideas and developmental plans. These are necessary functions of leadership. Nevertheless, nothing should be done without due consultation and input sessions. Wide counseling is always valuable to help leaders see any weaknesses in their plans, to offer any edification, additions or even reductions in plans. A wise leader will listen to the views of his colleagues.

At Hartland we have a plan whereby set reading is required of all constituents and board members. These are mainly Spirit of Prophecy books, yet there are a few other books especially related to Christian education, and doctrinal issues which have been made required reading. As all staff are members of the constituency, this reading is required of the staff. It is believed that all those in decision-making positions must have a clear vision of divine counsel so that rather than human decision making, decisions are founded upon the Word of God. Wide reading of divine counsel is a solid foundation for unity in decision making. The staff members also have another excellent opportunity to increase their knowledge. They may obtain from Hartland Publications, free of charge to them, any book published by Hartland Publications. The policy, however, requires active reading of books. Staff are permitted to take only one book at a time and must certify that they have read the book from cover to cover before they can access another book.

Also, there are times for staff with particular needs to consider attending conferences and seminars for the improvement of their understanding and skills. As finance is strengthening each year, a budget should be made which sets aside funds for staff to attend valuable seminars. Especially, those in technical areas such as computer-related technology, or skill areas in the health care or publishing industry, may, from time to time, benefit from such seminars. However, a self-supporting institution must always weigh the likely benefit of such seminars against the cost. Staff members should be required to provide convincing evidence of the necessity to attend the seminars and the benefits which they would derive from them. There are alternatives to costly seminars, conferences and training programs. Remember that the cost of a seminar goes beyond the registration fee. It also includes transportation, accommodation and meals. One question should be considered, Could not the staff obtain the information needed from recent books or other literature or from the world-wide web? The precious resources of a self-supporting institute should be carefully managed.

In many cases training seminars are available recorded on tape or CD. A library of these (a permanent asset of the ministry) may provide all or most of the benefits desired by staff members.

We must keep in mind that many worldly seminars are built upon pagan principles—principles of new-age thinking, of neuro-linguistic programming and other non-Christian concepts. It would not only be a culpable waste of God-given resources to send staff members to such seminars, it could very well subtly lead staff members to introduce worldly principles into God's institution.

SUMMARY

1 All staff need ongoing in-service training.
2 As much as possible, employ the resources of your own experienced staff to train less experienced staff.
3 First and foremost focus upon spiritual training in truth and righteousness.
  a. Staff meetings
  b. Worship, prayer meetings, and other spiritual services.
  c. Required reading especially in the field of ministry using inspired sources.
4 For upgrading skills and technical knowledge, there are books, magazines and web sites which will offer help at minimal cost to the institution.
5 If considering an expensive conference, seminar or training program, remember that the cost includes travel, accommodation and meal expenses. Recorded training may be available on the subjects sought.
6 Always weigh the possible benefits against the resources of the institution.
7 Many seminars and training programs are built upon pagan principles of mind control, Neurolinguistic Programs and New Age concepts. Do not waste time and resources on such training programs.

Chapter 24
Accreditations and Affiliations

MANY self-supporting institutions, especially those conducting educational facilities, will, somewhere along their journey, face the issue of what kind of affiliations would be acceptable to the Lord. Colin had served as president of an accredited Seventh-day Adventist denominational college—Columbia Union College—in the 1970s. It did not take long for him to determine that in spite of all the assurances otherwise, accreditation has been highly detrimental to the vision and goal of God's educational system. There are a number of ways in which accreditation compromises the divine philosophy. Even though it is claimed that the evaluation will be based upon the mission statement and goals of the institution, nevertheless, there are aspects of accreditation which cause institutions to compromise their purpose and their mission. These aspects include that—

1 Of four-year colleges it is required that at least forty percent of their professors have doctorates, and of universities, sixty percent. That is not an easy goal to achieve when one considers that our primary goals are to appoint staff who believe God's truth unwaveringly, are loyal to the Bible above any other authority, who live the Seventh-day Adventist message and are willing to sacrifice for it. We have concluded that most colleges, if not all, have compromised to achieve their goal that a minimum of forty or sixty percent of faculty have doctorates. Obviously this leads to the appointment of staff with high academic qualifications, but among whom are included some who will compromise the goals and the purposes of the institution and train young people away from the purposes for which the institution is established.

2   There is the inevitable requirement to add books and journals to the library. Often these are books in areas which we cannot accept, journals which contain material which is inimical to our goals. It may be possible at times to persuade the accrediting committee to delete such recommendations. Colin recalls a situation at Columbia Union College where the Maryland State Education Department Certification Team detailed the need to add adult literature to the library. Colin protested this before the report was finalized on the grounds that such literature was inimical to Christian values and to our goals. Colin succeeded in having the change made. However, the certifying team also asked that dance be added to the physical education program. This again Colin protested as inimical to the college's goals. When the final report was rendered, while dance was eliminated, they mandated that rhythm be added. Colin instructed the Chairman of the Physical Education Department at Columbia Union College that rhythm not be added to the curriculum, for he realized that step by step it could develop into dance. He hopes it never has been added since.

3   All changes mandated by Accreditation teams require additional funds. Considering the minimal resources which most self-supporting institutions have, this expense could easily bankrupt the institution. One of the classical examples of the deleterious effect of accreditation surely was Madison College, which was established as a model for all self-supporting colleges. It must have been an anguished Dr. Sutherland who eventually yielded to a controlling influence he knew to be inimical to the principles of heaven. He allowed a human organization to intervene between the Word of God and himself. One can understand the reasons for which Sutherland took this step but we can never condone that faulted decision.

Sutherland was a great Christian educator, maybe the

greatest this church has ever known. But the consequences of one wrong decision were tragic. Many years into the Madison experience Dr. Sutherland received a communication from his cofounder, Dr. Percy Magan, then the Administrator of the College of Medical Evangelists (now Loma Linda University). Dr. Magan informed Sutherland that unfortunately the College of Medical Evangelists could no longer continue to accept the graduates of Madison College into the medical program unless Madison College be accredited. It had been believed for many years that graduates from Madison College were given preference over graduates from Seventh-day Adventist denominational schools in the selection of entrants into Loma Linda Medical School. This had brought great prestige to Madison and the number of students increased until it reached about five hundred. This size was comparable to many of the denominational colleges at the time. No doubt Dr. Sutherland reasoned that should Madison graduates no longer be accepted into the medical program at Loma Linda, there would be a rapid decline in applications to attend Madison College; and this assumption may have been correct; but we must ever "trust in God and do the right thing."

The pressure was great, but the consequences of accreditation were fatal to the survival of the institution, and were to serve the purposes of Satan which led to the demise of this model institution. Madison's enrollment would no doubt have decreased unless God had specifically intervened. In any case, Madison was already nearly twice the size recommended by Sister White. She had declared that Battle Creek College was too large and had attracted too many families to locate near the college for the education of their children. She said that funds expended at Battle Creek should have been used to establish other smaller institutions. At the time Battle Creek had a student body of about one thousand—three times as large as inspiration had suggested.

> If two thirds of the people in Battle Creek were plants of the Lord in other localities, they would have room to grow. Greater results would have appeared if a portion of the time and energy bestowed on the large school in Battle

Creek to keep it in a healthy condition had been used for schools in other localities where there is room for agricultural pursuits to be carried on as a part of the education. Had there been a willingness to follow the Lord's ways and His plans, many plants would now be growing in other places. *Testimonies*, Vol. 6, 211, 212

Maybe Dr. Sutherland thought of the staff who would have to be released, or the lack of prestige that would ensure in such circumstances. This is a warning not to increase the size of an institution beyond that which will permit the effective training of the young people to be leaders at the end of time in the proclamation of the gospel to every nation, kindred, tongue and people.

It was the requirements of accreditation that led Madison College in 1963 to offer the college to the Southern Union Conference, and one year later for the college to be closed. Other institutions have opted for state approval or state authorization categories. We would strongly recommend against these as well. Every institution should make the commitment that they will listen to one voice and one voice alone, and that the voice of God. Of course, that does not mean that there should be no counseling with other godly people. The final Arbiter of what the end-time institutions must be, described by Sister White as schools "of an altogether different order from our older schools and colleges," expects us to follow the perfect guidelines of inspiration.

It is said that we can judge a man by his friends. There is much wisdom in this. But so also can an institution be judged by the other institutions with which from time to time it associates. We would recommend that every institution seek to work closely only with those who have unwavering loyalty to God and His truth. All institutions should be ready to work with any man or organization which has such loyalty, be they self-supporting or denominational. Remember that the great divide is today what it has always been—between God's faithful people and unfaithful people; between truth and error; righteousness and worldliness.

Discriminate between character and reputation. Our

characters must be jealously guarded. Remember that reputations are human opinions. Christ "made himself of no reputation" (Philippians 2:7). We must also be willing to be made of no reputation, if necessary that we might be faithful servants to God. There can be no compromise to garnish the reputation of an individual or institution. Do what is right and make God our defense. In so doing one day you will hear, "Well done, thou good and faithful servant; . . . enter thou into the joy of thy lord" (Matthew 25:21).

SUMMARY

1. Irrespective of assurances to the contrary, accreditation greatly compromises the vision and integrity of a Seventh-day Adventist institution.
2. Accreditation adds the pressure of high academic degrees when seeking to find faithful Seventh-day Adventist teachers.
3. Accreditation inevitably adds great additional costs, without substantially adding to the mission of the institution.
4. The history of both denominational and self-supporting institutions attests the perils of human accreditation.
5. Institutions must make the commitment to listen to one voice, and one voice alone, and that the voice of God.
6. Counseling widely with godly and experienced men and women can lead to discovering the will of God more fully.
7. Seek to work with other faithful ministries whether they be denominational or self-supporting.
8. Be careful not to link up with those who injure and compromise God's divine will.
9. All staff members must protect their characters but must be willing, if necessary, to lose their reputations rather than compromise God's ways.

Chapter 25
Moral Rectitude

IN OUR decadent age in which both Roman Catholic and Protestant clergy have been found guilty of vile sexual practices; and when many prominent churches such as the Uniting Church of Australia, (a union of the Congregationalist, Methodist and Presbyterian Churches), (July 2003), the Anglican Church of Britain (July 2003), and the Episcopalian Church of the United States (August 2003) have endorsed homosexual clergy, it is time for Seventh-day Adventists to shine as men and women of the highest moral standards.

Sadly, adultery is widespread among pastors and the laity, and homosexual practices are no barrier to church membership in some of our Seventh-day Adventist churches. There are, tragically, well-known churches which are a haven for practicing homosexuals.

The Bible is unequivocal: neither adulterer nor individual practicing homosexuals has, unless repentant and victorious over these sins, the slightest hope of salvation. It is not an act of love to condone these sins.

> Thou shalt not commit adultery. Exodus 20:14

> *Thou shalt not lie with mankind, as with womankind*: it is abomination. Leviticus 18:22, emphasis added

> If *a man also lie with mankind*, as he lieth with a woman, both of them have committed an abomination: they shall surely be put to death; their blood shall be upon them.
> Leviticus 20:13, emphasis added

> For this cause God gave them up unto vile affections: for even their *women did change the natural use into that which is against nature.* Romans 1:26, emphasis added

> Know ye not that the unrighteous shall not inherit the kingdom of God? Be not deceived: neither fornicators, nor idolaters, nor adulterers, nor effeminate, *nor abusers of themselves with mankind*, nor thieves, nor covetous, nor drunkards, nor revilers, nor extortioners, shall inherit the kingdom of God.
> 1 Corinthians 6:9, 10, emphasis added

> Knowing this, that the law is not made for a righteous man, but for the lawless and disobedient, for the ungodly and for sinners, for unholy and profane, for murderers of fathers and murderers of mothers, for manslayers, for whoremongers, for them *that defile themselves with mankind*, for menstealers, for liars, for perjured persons, and if there be any other thing that is contrary to sound doctrine.
> 1 Timothy 1:9, 10, emphasis added

In self-supporting work claims to piety are high. To work in God's self-supporting work in these last days is a sacred and holy privilege and an awesome responsibility. God requires the highest standard of conduct between self-supporting workers and those of the opposite sex.

> Holiness of heart will never lead to impure actions. When one who claims to be teaching the truth is inclined to be much in the company of young or even married women, when he familiarly lays his hand upon their person, or is often found conversing with them in a familiar manner, be afraid of him; the pure principles of truth are not inwrought in his soul. Such are not workers with Jesus; they are not in Christ, and Christ is not abiding in them. They need a thorough conversion before God can accept their labors. *Selected Messages*, Book. 2, 29—30

We live in an age when it is not men alone who make improper advances to those of the opposite sex; women are increasingly guilty of the same sin. Further, same-sex advances are increasingly common, as are acts of incest and pedophilia. All these are present in alarming levels in our beloved church. In these areas Satan destroys many erstwhile dedicated men and women. We must remember that,

> Moral pollution has done more than every other evil to cause the race to degenerate. *Testimonies*, Vol. 2, 391

Listen, and heed godly counsel.

> The subject of purity and propriety of deportment is one to which we must give heed. We must guard against the sins of this degenerate age. Let not Christ's ambassadors descend to trifling conversation, to familiarity with women, married or single. Let them keep their proper place with becoming dignity; yet at the same time they may be sociable, kind, and courteous to all. They must stand aloof from everything that savors of commonness and familiarity. This is forbidden ground, upon which it is unsafe to set the feet. Every word, every act, should tend to elevate, to refine, to ennoble. There is sin in thoughtlessness about such matters. *Gospel Workers*, 125

Notice God's warning directed to ministers concerning flattery.

> You will sometimes be flattered by men, but more frequently by women. Especially when you present the truth in new fields, will you meet persons who will engage in this wicked flattery. As a servant of Christ, despise the flattery; shun it as you would a venomous serpent. Rebuke the woman who will praise your smartness, holding your hand as long as she can retain it in her own. Have little to say to persons of this class; for they are the agents of Satan, and carry out his plans by laying bewitching snares to beguile you from the path of holiness. Every sensible Christian lady will act a modest part; she will understand the devices of Satan, and will not be a co-laborer with him. *Evangelism*, 679

No self-supporting worker should seek to establish ego and use sweet words to encourage women to fawn over him.

> Never earn the reputation of being a minister who is a

particular favorite with the women. Shun the society of those who by their arts would weaken in the least your purpose to do right, or bring a stain upon the purity of your conscience. *Ibid.*, 680

There is so much counsel on this matter that every worker must diligently study in order to live a life of absolute purity by the power of Christ.

> There should be connected with the mission married persons who will conduct themselves with the strictest propriety. But the danger is not alone from youth, but from married men and women; workers must build up the walls of modesty and virtue about themselves, so that women will not allure men, and men will not allure women, from strict propriety. 'Abstain from even the very appearance of evil.'. . .
>
> A man who claims to have believed present truth for years and is counted worthy by his brethren to fill positions of trust, in missions or in our institutions, may become careless when a change of circumstances brings him into temptations, and in his time he may tempt others. His case is sad indeed, for he reveals the workings of a corrupt heart, a want of that principle which every Christian should possess. When one who is entrusted with great responsibilities betrays his sacred trust and gives himself into the hands of Satan as an instrument of unrighteousness to sow the seeds of evil, corrupting the hearts and minds of others, he is a traitor of the worst type. From one such tainted, polluted mind the youth often receive the first impure thoughts that lead to a life of shame and defilement.
>
> If men placed at the head of a mission have not firmness of principle that will preserve them from every vestige of commonness, and unbecoming familiarity with young girls and women, after the light which has been so plainly given, let them be discharged without a second trial. There is a depravity of the soul which leads to these careless habits and practices, and which will far overbalance all the good such persons can do. We are living in an age of moral debasement; the world is as a second Sodom. Those who

Moral Rectitude

look for the coming of the Son of man, those who know that they are right upon the borders of the eternal world, should set an example in harmony with their faith. Those who do not maintain purity and holiness are not accepted of God. The true children of God have deep-rooted principles which will not be moved by temptations, because Christ is abiding in their hearts by faith.

A second trial would be of no avail to those whose moral sense is so perverted that they cannot see their danger. If after they have long held the truth, its sanctifying power has not established the character in piety, virtue and purity, let them be disconnected with the missions without delay: for through these Satan will insinuate the same lax sentiments in the minds of those who ought to have an example of virtue and moral dignity. Anything that approaches lovesick sentimentalism, any intimation of commonness, should be decidedly rebuked. One who is guilty of encouraging this improper familiarity should not only be relieved of responsibilities which he was unworthy to bear, but should be placed under censure of the church, and that censure should remain upon him, until he give evidence in spirit and deportment, that he sees his sinfulness and heart corruption, and repents, like any other guilty sinner, and is converted. Then God for Christ's sake will heal him of his transgression.
General Conference Daily Bulletin, February 6, 1893

Sadly, we are personally aware of at least twenty self-supporting workers, thirteen of them ministry leaders, who have fallen morally. A number of these failed self-supporting workers still dare to lead in ministries. While adultery is the commonest failing, homosexuality, pedophilia, serious indiscretions and incest have occurred in the ranks of self-supporting ministries. We must never believe that we are immune to this snare of Satan. Every morning we must yield ourselves to the Lord, plead for His character, His mind, His wisdom and His will. Daily we must seek the Holy Spirit in our lives. This alone is the strength of any self-supporting worker.

We also warn of another moral issue which is a growing concern in self-supporting work—embezzlement of ministry funds. It is time that we recognize that very shortly we will all need to give an account of every cent of ministry funds we have used. Further, there is evidence of the free use of means in some self-supporting ministries for that which serves self rather than the spread of God's message. Too often, motels are used when the individual has the offer of hospitality in a believer's home. Rental cars are frequently driven when a dear friend of God's work would happily supply an urgent transportation need. Remember the sin of Achan and its impediment to the work of God. Sister White states that every church has an Achan.

> If the presence of one Achan was sufficient to weaken the whole camp of Israel, can we be surprised at the little success which attends our efforts when every church and almost every family has its Achan?
> *Testimonies*, Vol. 5, 157

Do not be that Achan in your ministry!

It is our unwavering practice never to use money for personal benefits even if checks are written in our names. All funds received go into our ministries and are receipted to the donors. The Board of Directors of each institution determines the stipends of all the staff. This is to avoid even the hint that we are benefiting ourselves from the donors to the ministry. The highest quality of accounting procedures must be employed in each institution so that no loophole is left open. Make sure every transaction is totally transparent. We believe that such fiscal procedures protect both the ministry and ministry workers from any valid criticism.

SUMMARY

1. Moral lapses are among the most likely causes of the failure of both denominational and self-supporting workers.
    a. Do not become physically close to a member of the other sex.
    b. Avoid all light talk between males and females.

Moral Rectitude

    c. Keep close to Christ and commit the will to Him every morning.
    d. Do not flatter anyone, especially the opposite sex and do not allow flattery to charm you.
    e. Heed all divine counsels regarding working relationships with the opposite sex.
    f. Accept any warning counsel from all godly people. Do not continue in denial.
    g. Married workers must act with the strictest propriety.

2 Lack of financial integrity is also a strong cause for the failure of God's workers.
    a. Daily ask God for honesty and financial integrity.
    b. Never borrow funds without full financial transparency.
    c. Leaders especially must not consider that they have special privileges in financial matters. They must set the example.
    d. All self-supporting workers must practice frugality with the Lord's funds.
    e. If working in an institution make sure that you never solicit or use funds, even with your name on a check, for yourself. Make sure it is processed for use in the Institution.
    f. Leaders should not press for stipends much higher than other staff.
    g. Whenever possible save money, remembering it is easier to save than to solicit or earn funds.
    h. Make sure that all finances are subject to strict accounting principles and full transparency.

Chapter 26
Living and Working Together

ONE of the most effective ways in which Satan seeks to destabilize a ministry is by the rupture of interpersonal relations. Of course, there is no excuse among Christians for personal conflicts because God has given us many wonderful counsels to guide our pathway, to keep us from developing animosities, resentment and infighting. Most sizeable institutions have either all the staff, or a significant percentage of the staff, dwelling on the same campus. Therefore they are living in the same community. They are working together and, no doubt, are fellowshipping together in worship, chapel, prayer meetings, and vespers. For some institutions they also have a church on the campus. The staff may also be witnessing together. The high intensity of such a situation does allow Satan to work and seek to bring conflicts and divisions. If permitted, gossip and criticism develop rapidly.

These problems occur not only in self-supporting ministries, but also in the mission compounds associated with colleges and hospitals overseas. Satan will make certain that there are always decisions and initiatives which will not necessarily meet the mind of everyone in the institution. Of course, if those decisions are made contrary to the principles of the words of inspiration, then in Christian love this condition should be drawn to the attention of the one or ones who have made the decision so that it can be reversed. If the leaders are faithful servants of the Lord, they will acknowledge the mistake and redress it quickly.

Before approaching someone over a disagreement, pray

earnestly for the love of God in your heart before dialoging with that colleague. How different the results will be, than from an approach from a hasty tongue or angry heart.

> A soft answer turneth away wrath; but grievous words stir up anger. Proverbs 15:1

> By long forbearing is a prince persuaded, and a soft tongue breaketh the bone. Proverbs 25:15

We have found that earnest prayer never fails to endorse the admonition. Of course, if the issues are divine salvation principles which continue to be violated, then a decision needs to be made to serve in another ministry. However, most of the issues which cause irritation and stimulate gossip and criticism are not salvation issues.

Protocol should be set up in every institution to provide Christian guidelines of conduct in these areas. It is so easy for staff and/or administration to speak ill of one another and, of course, in the retelling even facts can become very distorted or exaggerated and minor matters magnified into major issues. In some self-supporting institutions there is a much greater emphasis upon the law than on love, when both are equally essential. They are among the many inseparable Siamese twins of the Bible, which include: faith and works, law and grace, justification and sanctification, justice and mercy, truth and sanctification. In separating any of these paired tenets both are destroyed.

It has been our experience that sometimes, but certainly not in the majority of cases, that spouses who are not in employment at the ministry develop a gossip ring where they pass around the tidbits (usually negative) which they glean from campus life. Staff should be counseled not to encourage anyone who is bringing negative gossip. Kindly, but firmly, the gossiper must be silenced; and the only way a gossiper is silenced is by the refusal of all others to listen to him or her. The reinforcement which gossipers receive from others convinces them that their words are right and their murmuring and complaining are justified. Such gossiping can lead to the vilification of some sincere members of the staff and may lead to resignations and an increased turnover of workers for the cause of Christ. Some become so disillusioned that they never again choose to serve the Lord in such a capacity. How grave the consequences can be.

However, there will be times when serious allegations or improprieties are brought to the attention of leaders. These have to be handled in special ways. Nevertheless, they must be handled in the ways of Christ. Generally speaking, secret investigations must be avoided. It is important to have appropriate protocol to address such situations. It is not wise to sweep these allegations under the rug. They should be thoroughly investigated, either to prove their validity or to exonerate the innocent. Here are some suggestions:

Have a fair and thorough strategy. Once that strategy is developed, then the one under investigation should be informed. At every level he should be present when the investigation is taking place. If there is a search of records, he should be there.

Colin once was confronted in a situation where two students came to him urging him to review a video of a class which had been presented by a Bible teacher. They claimed that he was very soft on one of the cardinal doctrines of the church. Colin explained to these young men that he certainly would not watch the tape without the professor being present. However, he would speak to the professor and ask him to watch the tape with him. This he did and it was true, in Colin's evaluation, that the teacher had not denied the truth but appeared to be saying that the error held by another man was of equal merit. Colin counseled the teacher to take up the issue again with the students and give the real strength that was needed to encourage the young people to believe truth and teach it with confidence.

If we are transparent in everything we do we will honor God. Of course, it is possible that some very serious accusations will be confirmed. It may be necessary to sever a staff member, a trainee or a student from the institute because of these situations. If one is found guilty of dishonesty, one must also be given the responsibility of restoring to the institution or person that which was stolen. However, the one to be dismissed must know that we still love him and that God has mercy for him. If with acknowledgement, confession, repentance and restoration, he petitions God, he can be brought back to his upright standing with God. Even when an individual is asked to leave, it should never be with the thought that harshness has been exercised or that there is no hope ever of returning.

Let us remind ourselves of the experience of Paul, Barnabas and John Mark. The tension was sharp between Paul and Barnabas.

> And the contention was so sharp between them, that they departed asunder one from the other: and so Barnabas took Mark, and sailed unto Cyprus. Acts 15:39

Paul was adamant. John Mark had failed the test of endurance under adverse circumstances, therefore he was judged unworthy to be a colleague in the important ministry which they were undertaking. Yet the same Paul, years later, could affirm the value of this man when he had proven his endurance in other projects.

> Only Luke is with me. Take Mark, and bring him with thee: for he is profitable to me for the ministry.
> 2 Timothy 4:11

No doubt John Mark had greatly matured and strengthened both his commitment to the Lord and his willingness to endure hardship for the gospel of Jesus Christ.

In dealing with an erring staff, trainee or student, do everything to restore such an one. Note the compassion and yet firmness of principle which Jesus employed when Mary Magdalene was cast at His feet, caught in the very act of adultery. She was a prostitute but in responding to her accusers, Jesus said,

> He that is without sin among you, let him first cast a stone at her. John 8:7

We have to realize that we are all fallen human beings and,

but for the grace of God, we would have no hope nor future in the world to come. This sinner was not condemned by Jesus.

> And Jesus said unto her, Neither do I condemn thee: go, and sin no more.   John 8:11

Paul expressed our responsibility to the erring one so well,

> Brethren, if a man be overtaken in a fault, ye which are spiritual, restore such an one in the spirit of meekness; considering thyself, lest thou also be tempted.
> Galatians 6:1

In dealing with a fallen human being we must also recognize that we are souls who also must guard vigilantly against being cast away.

> But I keep under my body, and bring it into subjection, lest that by any means, when I have preached to others, I myself should be a castaway.   1 Corinthians 9:27

Can we be joyous when someone stumbles under the fierce temptations of Satan?

> Rejoice not when thine enemy falleth, and let not thine heart be glad when he stumbleth.   Proverbs 24:17

In his love chapter Paul has counseled,

> Charity suffereth long, and is kind.
> 1 Corinthians 13:4

Judgment and justice must always be tempered with kindness and mercy. Perhaps one of the most amazing situations was that involving Christ's disciple, Peter. We have often wondered how we would have responded to Peter's conduct. Here at the greatest crisis, this braggart had boasted,

> Lord, I am ready to go with thee, both into prison, and to death.   Luke 22:33

But barely hours later he had fulfilled the prophecy of Jesus in denying his Lord. Note the words of the servant of the

Lord when commenting upon the terrible denial of Peter. Addressing the second accusation that Peter was a follower of Jesus, the servant of the Lord reported,

> At this Peter flew into a rage. The disciples of Jesus were noted for the purity of their language, and in order fully to deceive the questioners, and justify his assumed character, Peter now denied his Master with cursing and swearing. . . .
>
> While the *degrading oaths* were fresh upon Peter's lips, and the shrill crowing of the cock was still ringing in his ears, the Saviour turned from the frowning judges and looked full upon His poor disciple. At the same time Peter's eyes were drawn to his Master. In that gentle countenance he read deep pity and sorrow, but there was no anger there.
> *Desire of Ages*, 712, 713, emphasis added

As stated earlier, we wonder what we would have done. Here was a man who had denied his Savior. Here was a man who had used vile language. We feel that we would have dismissed him on the spot from the company of disciples. But a compassionate Savior desired to save him for His kingdom. Indeed, within a few weeks Peter became the courageous, mighty, spirit-filled preacher at Pentecost and went forward under the unction of the Holy Spirit to scatter the gospel of the kingdom to the world and indeed, eventually render up his life a martyr as a testimony to his unwavering loyalty to Jesus.

If we can help save men and women who may have fallen from the kingdom of heaven, that must be our goal.

SUMMARY

1 Staff living and working close to each other may face difficult personal relationships.
2 Murmurings, complaints, animosity and gossip far too often are found in campus life.
3 Pray earnestly for the love of Christ before approaching someone with whom you have a disagreement.

4. The administrators should establish protocol appropriate for the resolution of disputes, employing Christian principles.
5. Protocol also should be established for investigating serious allegations against a student, trainee or staff member.
6. Give the accused full understanding concerning the process of the investigation.
7. Wherever possible seek to save and restore the fallen.
8. Judgment and justice must be tempered with kindness and mercy. By so doing you may save such a one for greater service and for the kingdom of the Lord.

Chapter 27

Principles for Addressing the Erring

IT IS but rare in our fallen world that committees and boards achieve the perfect blend between justice and mercy in addressing disciplinary issues. For the lack of better words, some committees develop a permissive approach by appealing to the principles of individual freedom. They fall into Satan's traps by insisting that to uphold the high principles of heaven and the divinely mandated standards, they deprive others of their God-given freedom. In such circumstances, students and staff are neither taught nor admonished in the principles of God's protective standards. They are left to the practice of disobedience against the principles of heaven. Consequently, students and staff wallow in the polluted lifestyle and practice of the mores of corrupt society. Sadly this state of affairs is apparent in many Seventh-day Adventist institutions.

In the early days of our colleges and our Church history, God's standards were carefully followed. However, almost all colleges developed a legalistic, letter-of-the-law, rule-oriented mentality which, in the end, operated equally well to forward the destructive work of Satan. In such an environment souls are lost for eternity just as surely as in permissive colleges. In the end, this legalistic, letter-of-the-law approach becomes so obviously oppressive and crushing of the human spirit that there is an inevitable revolt against God's perfect principles and standards which are then tragically lowered. It begins first by turning a blind eye to some of the divine standards, and then follow actions which lead to specific changes in student and staff handbooks and church manuals. The consequences are eternal. Once God's standards are lowered, even a little, there is no end to the departure from God's protective shield to the shifting sand of fallible human reason until the standards bear almost no resemblance to the pure and holy principles of heaven.

Most who have attended Seventh-day Adventist schools decades ago will attest to this decline. The standards upheld in early times were consistent with the counsel from the Lord. These standards had remained essentially unchanged for decades. However, the education of the students detailing the inspired counsel and reasons for these rules was almost nil, yet the punishment for violators was usually quick and decisive. This experience was common to most of the earlier Seventh-day Adventist institutions. While the faculty could be content with "upholding the standards," quite a number of the students were victims of the stern, punitive methods which led to expulsion. Many of those expelled forsook their association with God's remnant church. Could there be a better way, a divinely ordained way? Yes, there is.

Such an approach was so unfair and so counterproductive, that somewhere during the following years, the divine principles and standards began to disappear. This drift to replace God's perfect principles with worldly, debased mores has not been arrested. The same trend can be seen to have developed in some self-supporting institutions. We believe that self-supporting institutions have the responsibility to follow not only the standards and principles of divine inspiration, but also the God-given method of handling those who fall short of these principles, whether staff or students.

The dynamics of committees and boards involves a very interesting and educative study. The differences between self-supporting and denominational work in this respect are very slight. God does not have different principles for one and not the other.

For self-supporting institutions to retain such high standards, they must constantly search for the divine paradigm and pray for ways to implement it. Often, new members of committees and boards have had little or no previous administrative experience. Usually, such new members are considerably less punitive in their approach because they are coming mostly from the thinking patterns of subordinate roles or from secular employment. However, a group-think mentality conceivably brings them into line with the well established patterns of operation. Committees seem to add rules to rules, ignoring Sister White's call for few rules.

> In the school as well as in the home there should be wise discipline. The teacher must make rules to guide the conduct of his pupils. These rules should be few and well considered, and once made they should be enforced. Every principle involved in them should be so placed before the student that he will be convinced of its justice.
> *Child Guidance*, 323

> Rules should be few and well considered; and when once made, they should be enforced. Whatever it is found impossible to change, the mind learns to recognize and adapt itself to; but the possibility of indulgence induces desire, hope, and uncertainty, and the results are restlessness, irritability, and insubordination.
> *Education*, 290

Staff of institutions need to seek continually and earnestly to evaluate every principle and decision by the Word of God, lest they be guilty of unwittingly falling into Satan's trap. Standing nobly for God's principles and standards is praiseworthy, but can we become legalistic and fail in compassion? We must remember that in the sphere of our influence, new institutions are being raised up by God and they will tend to look to earlier established institutions as their models. Avondale College, Australia, and Madison College, Tennessee, were established under the guidance of Sister White as pattern schools, and all later-established ministries should also be pattern institutions. However, the Word of God is to be the final authority. Staff members must make sure they are following God's principles in every way. It is easier and "safer" to administer rules by "the letter of the law," but—is that the way of Jesus? Paul says,

> Who also hath made us able ministers of the new testa-

ment; not of the letter, but of the spirit: for the letter killeth, but the spirit giveth life. 2 Corinthians 3:6

Sometimes those who seek a compassionate and merciful solution for violations of rules are perceived as "soft," "indulgent," "weak," and maybe unwilling to uphold God's standards and principles. It is feared that if mercy is extended, it will undermine the standards of an institution. Yet, the compassionate Savior never undermined the Decalogue or the divine principles. We must earnestly study these principles of handling the erring ones. Some, like Mary Magdalene, have by sin been robbed of any self-respect. Others, like Peter, are assertive, audacious and impulsive. Still others are selfishly ambitious, like James and John. But no matter what their personality characteristics, Christ dealt with them in such loving, compassionate mercy that their hearts were broken. Rather than undermining the laws and principles of His Father, Jesus established them. In the cases of Mary, Peter, James and John, their lives were saved and they ministered greatly for the kingdom as did others, such as Zacchaeus, the thief on the cross, and the Samaritan woman. Even those who ultimately turned away from the love of Jesus, such as the rich young ruler, Judas, and the second thief on the cross, Christ still extended His loving compassion to them.

What the letter-of-the-law cannot achieve, compassion and love may well accomplish. The drawing power of Christ can work the miracle of transformation in the life of the fallen sinner. We must study Christ's way and make it the only foundation of our practice.

The challenge is to uphold God's inviolate laws of life and conduct by a merciful, loving, restoring approach to the fallen one, while not sympathizing with, nor condoning the conduct which would lead to the lowering of God's principles and requirements. Sympathizing or condoning evil also does great hurt to the fallen one, and may lead him to resist reformation and hold harsh feelings against those who are, in love, pointing out character defects. It may lead to self-justification and even loss of eternal life.

Without the grace and mercy of Jesus, we would all be

helpless in the bondage of sin. As we have been forgiven, let us forgive others while never wavering from the divine principles and standards. Yet, we must recognize that there may be a time when the erring one shows no desire or evidence of reformation in his life. Sadly, that offending one may have to be removed. Even when such an action must be taken, let us express our genuine love for that person in word, and deed, and the hope that through the ministry of Christ and the Holy Spirit, such a one will one day stand with us by the sea of glass.

SUMMARY

1. Seek the blending of justice and mercy.
2. Liberals call lowering of God's standards, Freedom.
3. Legalism is the pitfall of conservatives.
4. Legalism inevitably leads to liberalism.
5. Early Seventh-day Adventist colleges often fell into the oppressiveness of legalism.
6. Only upholding God's principles in love leads to the maintenance of true Christian standards.
7. Many students, harshly treated, left the Seventh-day Adventist Church.
8. Avoid a group think mentality in committee.
9. Seek to restore the fallen.
10. Love and compassion are far more effective tools than letter-of-the-law enforcement.
11. Do not sympathize with, or condone the wrong deeds of the fallen.
12. Sometimes the erring one has to be removed.

Chapter 28

Dealing with Suspected Misconduct

1 Follow principles to solve personal differences and disputes.

> a. Therefore if thou bring thy gift to the altar, and there rememberest that thy brother hath aught against thee, leave there thy gift before the altar, and go thy way; first be reconciled to thy brother, and then come and offer thy gift. Matthew 5: 23, 24

> b. Many are zealous in religious services, while between them and their brethren are unhappy differences which they might reconcile. God requires them to do all in their power to restore harmony. Until they do this, He cannot accept their services. The Christian's duty in this matter is clearly pointed out. *Desire of Ages,* 311

> c. Moreover if thy brother shall trespass against thee, go and tell him his fault between thee and him alone: if he shall hear thee, thou hast gained thy brother. But if he will not hear thee, then take with thee one or two more, that in the mouth of two or three witnesses every word may be established. And if he shall neglect to hear them, tell it unto the church: but if he neglect to hear the church, let him be unto thee as an heathen man and a publican.
> Matthew 18:15–17

> d. The one who thinks that a teacher has done wrong should follow the directions given in the word: "If thy brother shall trespass against thee, go and tell him his fault between thee and him alone" (Matthew 18:15–17). Until this has been done, no one is justified in telling others of

Dealing with Suspected Misconduct

a brother's mistakes.
Counsel to Parents, Teachers, and Students, 154

2 Remember our own sins and failings when ministering to the erring ones.

a. So when they continued asking him, he lifted up himself, and said unto them, He that is without sin among you, let him first cast a stone at her. John 8:7

b. Let care and wisdom be shown when dealing with workers who, though they have made mistakes, have manifested an earnest, self-sacrificing interest in the work. Let their brethren say "We will not make matters worse by putting another in your place, without giving you opportunity to retrieve your mistake, and to stand on vantage ground, free from the burden of unjust criticism." Let them be given time to adjust themselves, to overcome the difficulties surrounding them, and to stand before angels and men as worthy workers. They have made mistakes, but would those who have questioned and criticized have done better? *Testimonies*, Vol. 7, 278, 279

c. But I keep under my body, and bring it into subjection: lest that by any means, when I have preached to others, I myself should be a castaway. 1 Corinthians. 9:27

3 Follow Bible rules and objectively listen to both sides.

a. None should allow their feelings of prejudice and resentment to be aroused by the relation of the wrongs of others; all should wait patiently until they hear both sides of the question, and then believe only what stern facts compel them to believe. At all times the safe course is not to listen to an evil report until the Bible rule has been strictly carried out. This will apply to some who have worked artfully to draw out from the unsuspecting, matters which they had no business with and which would do them no good to know. *Testimonies*, Vol. 5, 97

4 How to approach the erring one without partiality.

a. In almost every case where reproof is necessary, there will be some who entirely overlook the fact that the Spirit of the Lord has been grieved and His cause reproached. These will pity those who deserved reproof, because personal feelings have been hurt. All this unsanctified sympathy places the sympathizers where they are sharers in the guilt of the one reproved. In nine cases out of ten if the one reproved had been left under a sense of his wrongs, he might have been helped to see them and thereby have been reformed. But meddlesome, unsanctified sympathizers place altogether a wrong construction upon the motives of the reprover and the nature of the reproof given, and by sympathizing with the one reproved lead him to feel that he has been really abused; and his feelings rise up in rebellion against the one who has only done his duty. Those who faithfully discharge their unpleasant duties under a sense of their accountability to God will receive His blessing. *Testimonies*, Vol. 3, 359

b. Finally, be ye all of one mind, having compassion one of another, love as brethren, be pitiful, be courteous; not rendering evil for evil, or railing for railing, but contrariwise blessing; knowing that ye are thereunto called, that ye should inherit a blessing. 1 Peter 3:8–9

c. If a person is in error, be the more kind to him; if you are not courteous, you may drive him away from Christ. Let every word you speak, even the tones of your voice, express your interest in, and sympathy for, the souls that are in peril. If you are harsh, denunciatory, and impatient with them, you are doing the work of the enemy. You are opening a door of temptation to them, and Satan will represent you to them as one who knows not the Lord Jesus. They will think their own way is right, and that they are better than you. How then can you win the erring? They can recognize genuine piety, expressed in words and character. If you would teach repentance, faith, and humility, you must have the love of Jesus in your own hearts.
Testimonies to Ministers, 150, 151

d. Such hardness of heart, such a want of sympathy, such harshness is shown to those who are not special favorites, and it is registered in the books of heaven as a great sin. Many talk of the truth, they preach the theory of the truth, when the melting love of Jesus has not become a living,

active element in their character.
Testimonies to Ministers, 151

e. You may be just as severe and critical with your own defective character as you please, but be kind, pitiful, and courteous toward others. *Testimonies,* Vol. 5, 97

5 Do not be condemnatory or judgmental

a. She said, No man, Lord. And Jesus said unto her, Neither do I condemn thee, go and sin no more .
John 8:11

b. Her heart was melted and she cast herself at the feet of Jesus, sobbing out her grateful love, and with bitter tears confessing her sins. This was to her the beginning of a new life, a life of purity and peace, devoted to the service of God. In the uplifting of this fallen soul, Jesus performed a greater miracle than in healing the most grievous physical disease. He cured the spiritual malady, which is unto death everlasting. This penitent woman became one of His most steadfast followers. With self-sacrificing love and devotion she repaid His forgiving mercy.
Desire of Ages, 256–257

c. Judge not, and ye shall not be judged: condemn not, and ye shall not be condemned, forgive, and ye shall be forgiven. Luke 6:37

d. Do not criticize others, conjecturing as to their motives and passing judgment upon them.
Mount of Blessings, 124

e. For God sent not His Son into the world to condemn the world; but that the world through Him might be saved.
John 3:17

f. But Christ's mission was not for judgment but for salvation. *Desire of Ages,* 210

g. Therefore thou art inexcusable, O man, whosoever thou art that judgest: for wherein thou judgest another, thou condemnest thyself; for thou that judgest doest the same things. But we are sure that the judgment of God is according to truth against them which commit such things.

And thinkest thou this, O man, that judgest them which do such things, and doest the same, that thou shalt escape the judgment of God. Romans 2:1–3

h. Remember that soon your life record will pass in review before God. Remember, too, that He has said, "Thou art inexcusable, O man, whosoever art that judgest: ….for thou that judgest doest the same things.
Ministry of Healing, 485

i. And why beholdest thou the mote that is in they brother's eye, but considerest not the beam that is in thine own eye? Matthew 7:3

j. His words describe one who is swift to discern a defect in others. When he thinks he has detected a flaw in the character or the life he is exceedingly zealous in trying to point it out; but Jesus declares that the very trait of character developed in doing this un-Christlike work is, in comparison with the fault criticized, as a beam in proportion to a mote. It is one's own lack of the spirit of forbearance and love that leads him to make a world of an atom. Those who have never experienced the contrition of an entire surrender to Christ do not in their life make manifest the softening influence of the Saviour's love. They misrepresent the gentle, courteous spirit of the gospel and wound precious souls, for whom Christ died. According to the figure that our Saviour uses, he who indulges a censorious spirit is guilty of greater sin than in the one he accuses, for he not only commits the same sin, but adds to it conceit and censoriousness.
Mount of Blessing, 125

6 Avoid Gossiping

a. We think with horror of the cannibal who feasts on the still warm and trembling flesh of his victim; but are the results of even this practice more terrible than are the agony and ruin caused by misrepresenting motive, blackening reputation, dissecting character? Let the children, and the youth as well, learn what God says about these things: "Death and life are in the power of the tongue."

The spirit of gossip and the talebearing is one of Satan's

Dealing with Suspected Misconduct

special agencies to sow discord and strife, to separate friends, and to undermine the faith of many in the truthfulness of our positions. *Adventist Home*, 440, 441

b. A froward man soweth strife: and a whisperer separateth chief friends. Proverbs 16:28

c. Debate thy cause with thy neighbour himself; and discover not a secret to another. Proverbs 25:9

d. Speak not evil one of another, brethren. He that speaketh evil of his brother, and judgeth his brother, speaketh evil of the law, and judgeth the law: but if thou judge the law, thou art not a doer of the law, but a judge.
James 4:11

7 Avoid all evil surmisings.

a. ...strifes of words, whereof cometh envy, strife, railings, evil surmisings. 1 Timothy 6:4

b. There is nothing that so much retards and cripples the work in its various branches as jealousy and suspicion and evil surmisings. These reveal that disunion prevails among the workers for God. Selfishness is the root of all evil. *Evangelism*, 633

c. Many indulge freely in criticism and accusing. By giving expression to suspicion, jealousy, and discontent, they yield themselves as instruments to Satan. Before they realize what they are doing, the adversary has through them accomplished his purpose. The impression of evil has been made,. the shadow has been cast; the arrows of Satan have found their mark.
Christ's Object Lessons, 340–341

d. It is not the opposition of the world that most endangers the church of Christ. It is the evil cherished in the hearts of believers that works their most grievous disaster and most surely retards the progress of God's cause. There is no surer way of weakening spirituality than by cherishing envy, suspicion, faultfinding, and evil surmising. On the other hand, the strongest witness that God has sent His Son into the world is the existence of harmony and union

among men of varied dispositions who form His church. This witness it is the privilege of the followers of Christ to bear. But in order to do this, they must place themselves under Christ's command. Their characters must be conformed to His character and their wills to His will.
Acts of the Apostles, 549

8   When and how to rebuke

a. Them that sin rebuke before all, that others also may fear. 1 Timothy 5:20

b. The next morning, as we were about to leave for the house of worship to engage in the arduous labors of the day, a sister for whom I had a testimony that she lacked discretion and caution, and did not fully control her words, and actions, came in with her husband and manifested feelings of great unreconciliation and agitation. She commenced to talk and to weep. She murmured a little, and confessed a little, and justified self considerably. She had a wrong idea of many things I had stated to her. Her pride was touched as I brought out her faults in so public a manner. Here was evidently the main difficulty. But why should she feel thus? The brethren and sisters knew that these things were so, therefore, I was not informing them of anything new. But I doubt not that is was new to the sister herself. She did not know herself, and could not properly judge of her own words and acts. This is in a degree true of nearly all, hence the necessity of faithful reproofs in the church and the cultivation by all its members of love for the plain testimony.

Her husband seemed to feel unreconciled to my bringing out her faults before the church and stated that if Sister White had followed the directions of our Lord in Matthew 18:15-17 he should not have felt hurt: "Moreover, if thy brother shall trespass against thee, go and tell him his fault between thee and him alone: if he shall hear thee, thou hast gained thy brother. But if he will not hear thee, then take with thee one or two more, that in the mouth of two or three witnesses every word may be established. And if he shall neglect to hear them, tell it unto the church: but if he neglect to hear the church, let him be unto thee as an heathen man and a publican."

My husband then stated that he should understand that these words of our Lord had reference to cases of personal trespass, and could not be applied in the case of this sister. She had not trespassed against Sister White. But that which had been reproved publicly was public wrongs which threatened the prosperity of the church and the cause. *Testimonies*, Vol. 2, 14–15

c. Now we exhort you, brethren, warn them that are unruly, comfort the feebleminded, support the weak, be patient toward all *men.* 1 Thessalonians 5:14

d. Christ Himself did not suppress one word of truth, but He spoke it always in love. He exercised the greatest tact, and thoughtful, kind attention in His intercourse with the people. He was never rude, never needlessly spoke a severe word, never gave needless pain to a sensitive soul. He did not censure human weakness. He fearlessly denounced hypocrisy, unbelief , and iniquity, but tears were in His voice as He uttered His scathing rebukes.
Desire of Ages, 353

9 Forgiveness

a. Take heed to yourselves: If thy brother trespass against thee, rebuke him; and if he repent, forgive him. And if he trespass against thee seven times in a day, and seven times in a day turn again to thee, saying, I repent; thou shalt forgive him. Luke 17:3, 4

b. True confession is always of a specific character, and acknowledges particular sins. They may be of such a nature as to be brought before God only; they may be wrongs that should be confessed to individuals who have suffered injury through them; or they may be of a public character, and should then be as publicly confessed. But all confession should be definite and to the point, acknowledging the very sins of which you are guilty.
The Faith I Live By, 128

c. I saw that my husband had been too exacting toward those who were wrong and had injured him. He indulged

dissatisfied feelings, which could be of no benefit to the erring and could but make his own heart very unhappy.
Testimonies, Vol 1, 614

d. Too often when wrongs are committed again and again, and the wrongdoer confesses his fault, the injured one becomes weary, and thinks he has forgiven quite enough. But the Saviour has plainly told us how to deal with the erring: [Luke 17:4 quoted]. *Christ's Object Lessons*, 249

e. For if ye forgive men their trespasses, your heavenly Father will also forgive you: but if ye forgive not men their trespasses, neither will your Father forgive your trespasses.
Matthew 6:14, 15

f. We can receive forgiveness from God only as we forgive others. It is the love of God that draws us unto Him, and that love cannot touch our hearts without creating love for our brethren. *The Faith I Live By*, 131

g. He who is unforgiving cuts off the very channel through which alone he can receive mercy from God. We should not think that unless those who have injured us confess the wrong we are justified in withholding from them our forgiveness. It is their part, no doubt, to humble their hearts by repentance and confession; but we are to have a spirit of compassion toward those who have trespassed against us, whether or not they confess their faults.
Ibid.

h. Will you not, if any one has done you a wrong, and is too proud and stubborn to say to you, "I repent," go to the offender and say, "I love you for Christ's sake, and I forgive you the injury you have done me?" Jesus will witness and approve of this deed of love; and as you do to others, it shall be done again to you.
Sons and Daughters of God, 153

i. If a brother errs, forgive him if he asks you. If he is not humble enough to ask, forgive him in your heart, and express your forgiveness in word and action. Then the weight of his sin will not in any degree rest on you.
Review & Herald, April 8, 1902, ¶ 3

j. Nothing can justify an unforgiving spirit. He who is unmerciful toward others shows that he himself is not a partaker of God's pardoning grace.
The Faith I Live By, 131

k. We are not forgiven *because* we forgive, but *as* we forgive. *Ibid.*

10 Restoring the Fallen

a. Let all bitterness, and wrath, and anger, and clamour, and evil speaking, be put away from you, with all malice: and be ye kind one to another, tenderhearted, forgiving one another, even as God for Christ's sake hath forgiven you . Ephesians 4:31, 32

b. Cultivate a disposition to esteem others better than yourself. Be less self-sufficient, less confident; cherish patience, forbearance, and brotherly love. Be ready to help the erring, and have pity and tender sympathy toward those who are weak. You need not leave your business in order to glorify the Lord; but you may, from day to day, in every deed and word, while pursuing your usual avocations, honor Him whom you serve, thereby influencing for the right those with whom you are brought in contact.

Be courteous, tenderhearted, forgiving toward others. Let self sink in the love of Jesus, that you may honor your Redeemer and do the work that He has appointed for you to do. How little you know of the heart trials of poor souls who have been bound in the chains of darkness and who lack resolution and moral power. Strive to understand the weakness of others. Help the needy, crucify self, and let Jesus take possession of your soul, in order that you may carry out the principles of truth in your daily life. Then will you be, as never before, a blessing to the church and to all those with whom you come in contact.
Testimonies, Vol. 4, 133–134

c. Brethren, if a man be overtaken in a fault, ye which are spiritual, restore such an one in the spirit of meekness; considering thyself, lest thou also be tempted.
Galatians 6:1

d. Bear in mind that the work of restoring is to be our burden. This work is not to be done in a proud, officious, masterly way. Do not say, by your manner, "I have the power, and I will use it," and pour out accusations upon the erring one. Do your restoring "in the spirit of meekness; considering thyself, lest thou also be tempted." The work set before us to do for our brethren is not to cast them aside, not to press them into discouragement or despair by saying: "You have disappointed me, and I will not try to help you." *Testimonies*, Vol. 6, 398

e. Brethren if any of you do err from the truth, and one convert him; Let him know, that he which converteth the sinner from the error of his way, shall save a soul from death, and shall hide a multitude of sins.
James 5: 19, 20

f. Do not put him to shame by exposing his fault to others, nor bring dishonor upon Christ by making public the sin or error of one who bears His name. Often the truth must be plainly spoken to the erring; he must be led to see his error, that he may reform. But you are not to judge or to condemn. Make no attempt at self-justification. Let all your effort be for his recovery. In treating the wounds of the soul, there is need of the most delicate touch, the finest sensibility. Only the love that flows from the suffering one of Calvary can avail here. With pitying tenderness, let brother deal with brother, knowing that if you succeed, you will "save a soul from death," and "hide a multitude of sins." *Desire of Ages*, 440

g. But it is to the wrongdoer himself that we are to present the wrong. We are not to make it a matter of comment and criticism among ourselves; nor even after it is told to the church, are we at liberty to repeat it to others. A knowledge of the faults of Christians will be only a cause of stumbling to the unbelieving world; and by dwelling upon these things, we ourselves can receive only harm; for it is by beholding that we become changed. While we seek to correct the errors of a brother, the Spirit of Christ will lead us to shield him, as far as possible, from the criticism of even his own brethren, and how much more from the censure of the unbelieving world. We ourselves are erring, and need Christ's pity and forgiveness, and just as we wish Him to deal with us, He bids us deal with one another. *Desire of Ages,* 441

SUMMARY

1. Personal differences should be resolved one-on-one.
2. Only if this fails should the rest of Matthew 18:15–17 be applied.
3. Remember our own sins when dealing with the sins of others.
4. Remember to make no decisions until having listened objectively to both sides.
5. Approach the erring one without partiality.
6. Never be condemnatory or judgmental.
7. Avoid gossiping.
8. Avoid all evil surmising.
9. Rebuke publicly only when the sin is public knowledge.
10. Forgive another even when such forgiveness is not asked for.
11. Restoring the fallen should be the burden of us all.

Chapter 29
Applying Biblical Principles

A. *HOW TO RESPOND TO PERSONAL DIFFICULTIES*

1 Before approaching another on a sensitive issue, pray earnestly for God to give you a deep love for that soul for whom Christ died.
2 Search your own heart to be sure that your motives are free from any personal negativity or bias.
3 Rehearse the positive qualities of that individual.
4 When at all possible avoid use of letters, faxes, e-mails or telephones to address sensitive issues. It is always best to follow the Biblical principle of face-to-face communication.
5 Pray earnestly together one for the other before any dialogue begins.
6 Make reconciliation and restoration a primary goal of your dialogue. Make it as easy as possible for an erring one to determine to seek spiritual recovery.
7 Do not permit anyone to dialogue in an unfavorable manner with you concerning another unless you have ascertained that the one seeking to dialogue has followed all the Biblical steps without success.
8 When forgiveness has been sought and a full reconciliation has been achieved, this should be the end of all communication on the issue.
9 *Never* form a judgment on hearing only one side of a situation.

B. STEPS IN DEALING WITH THOSE SUSPECTED OF MISCONDUCT

1   Staff with interpersonal disputes.

   a. Staff must be encouraged to resolve their own interpersonal disputes quickly.

   b. No one should consent to act as a go-between in an interpersonal dispute until the two parties have sought a prayerful solution to their dispute.

   c. Urge both parties to use divine principles to settle the dispute.

   d. Do not widen the circle to any additional persons.

   e. If one has wronged others or others have been offended by him or her, the matter must be made right. If the wrong is a public matter it must be confessed publicly and forgiveness sought. All such wrongs must be confessed as privately as possible and as widely as necessary.

   f. If all of the above efforts fail, bring the disputing parties together to explain that their unresolved disputes threaten the loss of God's blessing not only upon themselves, but also upon the institution.

   g. Reiterate divine principles for a solution and assure the two parties of your earnest prayers for them.

   h. Only if this approach fails, bring the divisional leader(s) to encourage the disagreeing parties to follow God's principles.

   i. If ultimately, both or one refuse to reconcile for the sake of God's work, they or the one refusing may have to be separated from the institute; however they must be assured that such a move is done in genuine love and there will be continued prayer for them.

2   Staff suspected of dishonest, immoral, or other un-Christ-like conduct.

   a. If a staff member is suspected of a serious lapse such as immorality, dishonesty, use of profane language, serious physical assault; the division leader, or if the accused be a division leader, the president must address the one suspected, presenting to him or her the preliminary evidence. Staff may choose one staff member or spouse to be present with him/her if further dialogues are needed.

b. When a division leader receives preliminary evidence concerning a staff member, the staff member is to be informed fully of the evidence in the presence of the one presenting that evidence. If the issues are financial, the treasurer should be present. In other cases, the President should be present. If the President is suspected, the Board Chairman should be present.

c. Absolute confidentiality must be maintained. Only the ones who have the responsibility to investigate the situation should be involved or informed.

d. After a thorough investigation, if the objective evidence against the accused is strong, and efforts to restore have failed, and if the situation is gravely serious, the accused should be given the opportunity to withdraw from the Institution. If he or she decides not to withdraw, the matter should be placed before the Board if an Administrator, or the Administrative Committee if a staff member, for a decision to be rendered. In such a hearing the accused must be afforded the opportunity to be present at the hearing and given the opportunity to respond to the accusation. There should be no others informed of the situation than those involved or have knowledge prior to the investigation. If it is determined that the accused is guilty as charged, an appropriate action should be assessed, always keeping in mind a priority goal for the restoration of the fallen one.

e. Any appeals made by the one disciplined end at the highest level of the organization.

f. If accusations have proven to be malicious, the accuser must face disciplinary procedures.

g. If the evidence proves the accusations false, or if the evidence is insufficient or inconclusive, the accused is to be exonerated and confirmed in his or her institutional role with appropriate encouragement in his or her ministry.

h. The widening of the circle to others not involved in the process will be treated as a serious breach of biblical ethics and the one responsible will be open to disciplinary action by the appropriate body.

3   Addressing doctrinal deviations by staff or administrators.

    a. Speculative ideas, those ideas which do not bear the divine authority of a "plain thus saith the Lord," should not be spread on campus. Staff must refrain from sharing their speculative views with fellow staff and/or students.

    b. There can be no tolerance of pluralistic interpretations of fundamental biblical doctrines, such as the three angels' messages, the sanctuary message, the Sabbath, the state of the dead, righteousness by faith, the fallen human nature of Christ, the eternal existence of Christ, character perfection, historicist interpretation of prophecy, the binding commandments of the law of God, the three-Member Godhead, believer's immersion baptism, the papal antichrist. Winds of doctrine such as feast-day keeping, the Wednesday crucifixion, compulsory use of the Hebrew names of God, rejection of the three-Person Godhead and other such winds of doctrine cannot be held or practiced.

    c. Minor interpretations of non-salvational issues which are not clearly revealed in inspiration, such as the seven heads of Revelation 17, the glorious holy mountain of Daniel 11, will be treated differently. Staff should have some freedom on such topics. However, wisdom dictates that such beliefs be not presented as vital testing truths or used to confuse and divide students or staff. The servant of the Lord has counseled that issues such as details of the 144,000, the law in Galatians, the "daily" of Daniel 8 should not be permitted to divide God's people.

    d. All the principles in paragraph B, 2b must be applied in addressing, staff members or administrators suspected of sharing views opposed to the pillars of the Bible such as the Sanctuary message, the Sabbath, the law of God, the state of the dead, the immortality of the soul, believers' baptism, righteousness by faith.

4   Students suspected of dishonest, immoral, or other un-Christlike conduct.

a. The Chairperson of the department or one of the deans must inform the student of the concerns.

b. If necessary, the chairperson of the department with the head of the academy or college and the appropriate dormitory Dean will conduct the investigation. Nothing is to proceed without the presence of the student suspected of wrong doing.

c. Absolute confidentiality must be maintained. No other individual should be involved, unless it be absolutely necessary, and that at the approval of the head of the educational institution..

d. If, after a thorough investigation, the evidence proves strong, then follow the same principles as enunciated in paragraph B, 2d. The student should be given the opportunity to withdraw from school. If the student declines, the matter should be placed before the Citizenship Committee for a decision to be rendered. In such a hearing the accused must be afforded the opportunity to be present at the hearing and be given the opportunity to respond to the accusations.

e. Dismissal should be reserved for only the most serious situations.

f. If the accusations prove false, insufficient, or inconclusive, there should be no widening of the knowledge of the situation to others. The student should be exonerated, encouraged in his training for the Lord's service, and permitted to continue his /her studies.

SUMMARY

1 If possible, issues should be handled privately.
2 Serious questions of misconduct should be handled as privately as possible.
3 The restoration of the erring one must always be a primary goal. Yet, the integrity of God's principles and the integrity of His institution must constantly be upheld.
4 Remember that handling an issue in an un-Christlike fashion will inevitably be the forerunner of the lowering of God's principles and standards, as the history of other

schools attest.
5. Breaking confidentiality is a major violation of Biblical and Spirit of Prophecy ethics and the suspected offender will face disciplinary proceedings consistent with the principles established by God's standards.
6. As far as possible, the problems should be treated with the same protection appropriately afforded to family and church problems. They should not be spread to those not involved.

Chapter 30
Why God-Raised-Up Institutions Fail

ONE of the most sober studies which we have undertaken is to research some of the most notable ministries established by God in the history of the world. We have come to the realization that *all* such ministries, without exception, have ultimately failed and been derailed by Satan. Here are some examples:

1 *The Eden School*

In spite of a perfect environment and pupils who had no bent to sin and evil; in spite of the fact that Adam and Eve had daily communion with angelic beings and frequent communion with Christ Himself, the school was a failure. Indeed it had a one-hundred percent failure rate. The failure was so all-encompassing that the whole of the physical and vegetative world, the creatures of the world and the human race were infected by sin. The nature of all creation was blighted. The sin of Adam and Eve is the best illustration of how terrible are the consequences of one sin. This failure was not the fault of God any more than the failure of one-third of the angels in heaven was God's fault. It resulted from a choice to accept the words of the father of lies, Satan, and thus reject the word of God.

2 *The Patriarchal Schools*

After the fall of Adam and Eve, the patriarchs (normally the oldest son in each generation), upon the death of the father, became the patriarch. The patriarch was to be not only the father, but the educator of all under his care, and was appointed to be the great spiritual leader of the next generation. He was priest, educator and legislator. This system continued among God's people until the time of the Egyptian captivity where, under the oppression of the Egyptians, it disappeared.

3   The Mosaic Educational System

At the time of the exodus, Moses was not only the leader of Israelites, but also a prophet, who established one of the most extensive educational systems devised in the world. It covered in great detail the spiritual life of the Israelites. The civil and moral laws, the laws of health and hygiene and many other laws were established by God. Yet this system of education disintegrated when, against the very counsel of the Lord, many of the Israelite men married pagan women. These women, not knowing the true God or the Word of God, trained the children in pagan practices and, tragically and inevitably, the Mosaic educational system also failed.

4   The Schools of the Prophets

The first two schools of the prophets were established by Samuel and they became very prominent in the time of the prophets Elijah and Elisha. They were established to educate chosen young men to be leaders.

> The schools of the prophets were founded by Samuel to serve as a barrier against the wide-spread corruption, to provide for the moral and spiritual welfare of the youth, and to promote the future prosperity of the nation by furnishing it with men qualified to act in the fear of God as leaders and counselors. In the accomplishment of this object. Samuel gathered companies of young men who were pious, intelligent, and studious.
>
> Patriarchs and Prophets, 593

These schools were established to train young men to go back into Israel and turn the Israelites away from the idolatry which they had accepted.

> These schools were intended to serve as a barrier against the wide-spreading corruption, to provide for the mental and spiritual welfare of the youth, and to promote the

prosperity of the nation by furnishing it with men qualified to act in the fear of God as leaders and counselors.
Education, 46

The sad thing is that these schools failed also. We hear nothing about the sons of the prophets after the death of Elisha.

5 *The Schools of the Restoration*

After the Babylonian captivity, synagogue schools were raised up to train all the children of Judah. Also, rabbinical schools were established. Soon it was considered a disgrace if a synagogue did not have a school attached to it. While rabbinical schools were designed to help in training the leaders for their responsibility in the work of God, how miserably they failed. Elder F. C. Gilbert, a converted Jew, explains why these schools failed, thus leading the Jews to reject their Messiah when He came to earth.

> An arrangement was entered into that allowed a large number of rabbis from Jerusalem to go to Alexandria and translate the writings of the Jewish Scriptures into the Greek language. . . . It was also suggested by the Greeks that the Jews send their talented young men to Alexandria for training and instruction in the philosophies, sciences, and learning of the Greeks.
>
> Many of the elders of Israel feared the results of such a course; the sages remembered the sorrows of their ancestors who came into contact with heathen manners and customs. They counseled the younger men against such a procedure. These, in turn, argued that it would be an advantage for strong, thoughtful, vigorous young men to enter the schools of Greece, as they might influence the philosophers and Greek scholars to see the value and beauty of the Jewish religion, and some of the learned Greeks might embrace Judaism. Yet the aged men of Israel advised against it. They maintained that should the younger men be given encouragement to come into contact with the learning of the heathen, it might be ruinous to the future of the Jewish race.

Why God-Raised-Up Institutions Fail

Greece assured the fathers in Israel that they might hold to their own standards of religion. They were encouraged to believe that the synagogues where the children were taught their religion would not be interfered with; their *Beth Hamedrosh* (house of learning, their high schools), where their young people received a preparatory training, would continue as heretofore; the *Talmus Torah* (their colleges where advanced studies were conducted) would be strengthened if the teachers of the law should only imbibe the wisdom and learning of the scholars of Greece; and by receiving recognition from the world's greatest nation, the graduates of Jewish schools would find it greatly to their advantage.

Many of Israel's influential men yielded to Greek insistence. The former said that God would help their young men to be true to their religion, and the training schools of Jewry would have a better standing in the eyes of the nations. . . .

Gradually the Jewish schools came to confer degrees upon their graduates. . . . It was thought necessary for the graduates of the rabbinical schools to show the mark of their rank by wearing different clothing. . . . Little by little an educational aristocracy was formed, which was called the Sanhedrin. . . .

While the religious schools continued to operate, a marked declension in spiritual influence and power was visible. Year by year the word of God was studied less, as the courses of studies based on culture and philosophy increased. The curriculum of the rabbinical schools was influenced toward intellectualism. As the years passed, man became exalted and God was less thought of. The rabbi was extolled; the unlearned were depreciated. Piety gradually diminished as form and ceremony increased. . . .

In order for men to be accepted by Jewish assemblies, they must have completed a course in the rabinical schools. Those who failed to follow the procedure mapped out by the Great Sanhedrin . . . received no recognition by the populace. The graduate rabbi was known by his garb. It was vital that rabbinical qualifications be met in order for a person to gain a hearing by the children of Abraham.

Such were existing conditions in the land of Judea at the time when John and Jesus appeared in the land of Israel.

The following from "The Desire of Ages" is pertinent here:

"As they departed from God, the Jews in a great degree lost sight of the teaching of the ritual service. . . . In order to supply the place of that which they had lost, the priests and rabbis multiplied requirements of their own; and the more rigid they grew, the less of the love of God was manifested. They measured their holiness by the multitude of their ceremonies, while their hearts were filled with pride and hypocrisy. –Desire of Ages, 29

"As the Jews had departed from God, faith had grown dim, and hope had well-nigh ceased to illuminate the future. The words of the prophets were uncomprehended."
Ibid., 32

. . . Because the standards of learning were set up by the Sanhedrin, and none who refused to accept the teaching of the rabbis were given recognition, it is not difficult to understand why, when the Saviour came to those who were custodians of the oracles of God, they failed to recognize Him as the fulfillment of the types and prophecy noted in Moses and the prophets. By mingling human philosophy with the word of God, the spiritual force and power of the Scriptures was lacking in the lives of teacher and layman. . . .

The leaders of Israel had, to a great extent, yielded to the demands of Greek culture and learning, thereby hoping to gain prestige and influence. They had been led to believe that they could make better progress in their God-given task by assimilating worldly standards of education than by clinging with tenacity to the old standards bequeathed to them by their godly ancestors. So the Israelites lost much of their influence, failed to retain their prestige, and rejected their long-looked-for Messiah and Saviour. (F. C. Gilbert, "Why The Jews Rejected Jesus as the Messiah"; *Ministry Magazine*, Dec. 1933, 14, 15, 22, 23.)

The failure of these schools was complete.

6   *The Early Christian Schools*

After some time, Christian schools were established. By the second and third century there were quite a number of them. Some were called cathedral schools, where cathedrals would establish educational training for some of the young people. Some were called song schools, schools where the members of the boys choir would be educated. Others were called catechistic schools, which trained children in the teachings of the church although, by this time these teachings were quite polluted. Some were called Monastic schools and others Convent schools. However, all of them were very quickly compromised by the intrusion of paganism into the Christian faith.

One of the most famous schools was established in the second century in Alexandria, Egypt, but almost immediately the leaders, such as Clement and Origen, refused to take the Bible as it read, interpreting it through the eyes of Greek pagan philosophers. Needless to say they not only failed, they destroyed the purity of God's truth. They also tampered with the New Testament writings, thus corrupting them. These Greek manuscripts became known as the Western Alexandrian texts which, sadly, are now used for most of the modern Bible translations instead of the reliable Eastern Syrian Greek manuscripts. (See Russell & Colin Standish, *Modern Bible Translations Unmasked*.)

7   *The Celtic Schools*

The Celtic schools were established in the British Isles. One of the most famous Celtic schools was Iona, established by the Irish prince Columba on the island of Iona, off the wind-swept west coast of southern Scotland. For about six hundred years this great school sent out missionaries not only into Britain, but onto the continent as well.

The second such school was established by Aidan, a

graduate from Iona. He established his school in Lindisfarne, off the east coast of northern England. Other great leaders included Coleman and abbess Hilda and a little later, Caedmon. A third cluster of famous schools were established by Dinooth in northern Wales near what is now the city of Bangor. Indeed Dinooth founded seven seminaries near Bangor, training young people for the ministry with none less than three hundred students. At any time there were up to two thousand five hundred young men training in these Bangor schools.

The most famous graduate of Donooth's schools was Columbanus, who led a party of fourteen to Luxor in France and into the primeval forest where they had to contend with the wolves and bears. By the grace of God, they survived the rigors of the first winter, sometimes eating bark, but eventually they were supported by the king of a small territory, King Guntram, ruler of Burgandy. (See B. G. Wilkinson, *Truth Triumphant*, 175, 176). Columbanus later raised up schools in what are now Germany and Austria. The final school he established before his death was in Bobbio in northern Italy. However, under the ruthless persecution of the Roman Catholic Church against these Christians who would not accept their papal errors, the Celtic missionaries disappeared by the ninth or tenth century.

8 *The Schools of the Waldensians*

The Waldensian school was established to train young men, at the risk of their lives, to go down into the valleys and trade as merchants while seeking to find those who would be willing to study the Word of God. This was a very solemn training of these young men. Of course, some of them never returned. Either they were imprisoned or martyred. Some, no doubt, were tortured. The Waldensians lost their faithful witness when eventually the Waldensians voted to send their children to the Reformation school in Geneva which trained them in the Calvinistic theology. In one or two generations they had lost the basic beliefs which their fathers had cherished for centuries, and embraced the impotent, unscriptural Calvinistic concepts of predestinarian salvation.

9 The Schools of the Reformation

It was a dictum of the Reformers that every boy and girl should be educated to read and to write so that they could understand the Bible for themselves, in order that they would not be dependent upon priest or prelate to explain to them the Word of God. There were many great educators—Comenius (Komensky), the last bishop of the Moravian Brethren, a wonderful educator who sought to bring education to all the young people in what is now the eastern part of the Czech Republic. Melancthon, the right-hand man of Luther, established a very strong educational system. Calvin, himself, raised up schools. One of the greatest educators of the Reformation was John Knox in Scotland. His plan was to have what we would call an elementary school with every parish, a high school with every diocese, and a university in every archdiocese. While he did not achieve that goal, nevertheless, he went a long way toward it, and at that time education in Scotland was far in advance of the education available in England. In the early nineteenth century Scotland had five medical schools, while England had only two—Oxford and Cambridge. These schools of the Reformation inspired the schools in the new world and many of the early training institutions of America were patterned upon these Reformation schools, none more important than Harvard. However, they were compromised by humanism and secularism and soon were far removed from the noble goals of their founders.

10 The Schools of the Seventh-day Adventist Church

It was only to be expected that the great reformatory movement envisaged by the three angels' messages and the everlasting gospel would soon lead to the establishment of a school system. Indeed, it was the Seventh-day Adventist school system which was to become the largest school system of any denomination around the world with the exception of the system of the Roman Catholics. It began with elementary schools, followed by colleges and then by secondary schools. Like the schools which had come before them, they had a responsibility to train and educate children and youth in the mighty truths which were espoused by the pioneers of the church and endorsed by the Spirit of Prophecy. Sadly, today around the world we see the telltale change both in the doctrinal teaching and in the goals and purposes of these schools. As recently acknowledged, the mission and purpose of denominational schools have been seriously compromised by secularism.

11 *Seventh-day Adventist Self-Supporting Schools*

To fill the increasing educational void, created by the significant loss of direction in the denominational schools, new self-supporting schools are being established. These schools are to be established after the patterns which God has given to us in Avondale (denominational) and Madison Colleges (self-supporting) at their beginning. These new schools are being raised up as the fulfillment of prophecy.

> The plan of the schools we shall establish in these closing years of the message is to be of an entirely different order from those we have instituted.
> *Counsels to Parents, Teachers, and Students*, 532

These are not schools established after the pattern of the world nor patterned after those schools established in our past history, but they are patterned upon the Eden school, the schools of the prophets and upon the school of Christ. Yet they also run a great danger of being derailed by Satan. Satan is a determined fallen angel and every effort will be sustained by him to bring even small defection from the paradigm which God has set before us. It is essential that those who establish any institution realize that that institution in one way or another is an educational institution, whether it be directly a school at any level of instruction, or a health center, a publishing work, a tape/video ministry or whatever it may be. Each such ministry is established to educate those who are enrolled with the pure gospel of Jesus Christ which will lead men and women to eternal salvation.

We must recognize that many institutions do not retain the biblical vision, goals and purposes of the original leaders, and very rarely do they maintain the goals after the second leader. For example, there were Moses and Joshua, successive faithful leaders of the Lord. But what happened after them?

Why God-Raised-Up Institutions Fail

There is a sad record in Scripture of what happened. Notice the prophecy of Moses and subsequent Scriptural records.

> For I know that after my death ye will utterly corrupt yourselves, and turn aside from the way which I have commanded you; and evil will befall you in the latter days; because ye will do evil in the sight of the Lord, to provoke him to anger through the work of your hands.
> Deuteronomy 31:29

> And Israel served the Lord all the days of Joshua, and all the days of the elders that overlived Joshua, and which had known all the works of the Lord, that he had done for Israel.
> Joshua 24:31

> And the people served the Lord all the days of Joshua, and all the days of the elders that outlived Joshua, who had seen all the great works of the Lord, that he did for Israel.
> Judges 2:7

Sadly, Moses' prophecy was fulfilled sometime after the death of Joshua.

Another example is Elijah/Elisha. When Elisha fades from the record of Scripture so too do the schools of the prophets. Perhaps they continued for a short while. But certainly something happened that led to their failure and ultimate disappearance.

We have often contemplated, "How is it that every God-established institution has been derailed by Satan's persistent efforts?" Maybe we can learn a lesson from the world of finance. This may seem a strange place to look for a solution, for surely we all agree that the foundation of all truth is the Word of God. However, it was Jesus who said,

> . . . for the children of this world are in their generation wiser than the children of light.
> Luke 16:8

An article by Morgan Witzel, entitled "The Chronicler of Greatness," was reported in the *Financial Times*, August 18, 2003. The article was written concerning Jim Collins, a former professor at Stanford University. Collins, over the years has done an in-depth study of why good companies eventually become enduring great companies. He investigated how such companies grow and how they attain to greatness. His first statement would seem like common sense—maybe common sense too little exercised,

> That takes a combination of vision, tenacity, discipline and skill, and companies that lack these will not make the grade. *Ibid.*

Just as companies without a clear and decided vision have little chance of success, so self-supporting institutions without a clear and well-defined vision are likely to fail.

> The key to survival for great companies is an enduring vision. That vision must belong to the organization as a whole: visionary leaders pass on, and so-called great ideas never last. Organizational vision is not built around a person or a product—they both may be important in the original creation of the vision—but around an ideology which says what the organization's purpose [is]. Professor Collins and Professor Porras [his colleague] argued that "visionary companies succeed because their core ideology remains unshaken despite changes around them. *Ibid.*

What a wonderful insight for lay and self-supporting workers. Surely the failure of all God-raised-up institutions of the past is that their God-given vision and their original ideology have faltered in the face of changing sociological, political and economic mores in society. The present generation is making the same tragic mistake. Bible and Spirit of Prophecy principles are everlasting, and we must be unwavering to the vision and ideology God has entrusted to us. We must not establish such an institution until all who are part of the institution have studied in depth, and are united by, the vision which God has provided and the ideology from His Word.

How does that relate to self-supporting ministries? Our vision must be built exclusively upon the principles of the Bible and the Spirit of Prophecy. They must not be dependent upon one man or woman or even a group of men and women. They must be ingrained within the beliefs and practices of all

Why God-Raised-Up Institutions Fail

who are part of the ministry. Each individual has a responsibility to see that absolutely *no* ideological changes contrary to inspiration come into the ministry.

We do not want to be misunderstood, however, about the importance of an unwavering ideology built on the divine principles of God. This is not to be interpreted as the institution developing a complacency with the status quo. On the contrary, while the vision must not change unless we have found some area where we have been inconsistent with the divine principles of God, nevertheless there must always be advancement. God is not a God of the status quo and neither can self-supporting workers be satisfied with the status quo. Indeed, those who are satisfied that they have achieved their goals are then placed in a very dangerous situation. We believe there is no plateauing of ministry. It must move ever forward, onward, while ever expanding. So while the vision remains unwavering, the scope of the institution must continue to expand. If we do not expand and press forward, almost certainly the institution will go into decline and eventually be at risk of faltering and maybe failing. Let us ever remember the lesson from the Madison College experience. The Bible is very plain that at this time we must be pressing forward as never before. Our philosophy must be "While I live I grow and while I grow I live."

> Enlarge the place of thy tent, and let them stretch forth the curtains of thine habitations: spare not, lengthen thy cords, and strengthen thy stakes.   Isaiah 54:2

Now, as never before, we are to lengthen the cords and strengthen the stakes. This can be achieved only by pressing forward and earnestly entreating the Lord to prepare our hearts and lives for the reception of the latter rain. Every individual, family and institutional ministry must press forward with a divine vision and ideology and the same earnest endeavors.

At Hartland, for example, we started with a vision to follow the Lord, and Him alone. This led us to seek to establish a college and a wellness center. Subsequent to that the Lord has expanded our mission to include the publications work and to establish the division of world mission. The unwavering vision has remained, focusing all efforts of the institution upon the preserving of the infallible truths of the Word of God, the salvation of men and women for the kingdom of heaven and the spread of the gospel around the world by every means possible.

Highwood in Australia, established more than twenty years after Hartland, was able to learn from Hartland's experience. It commenced twenty years nearer to Christ's coming, so its training course is only one year in duration to stress the urgency of the times. It commenced with five areas of service—Highwood Health (wellness program), Highwood College (a single course of training in evangelism of all forms including health and education), Highwood Family (camps including junior and youth, home-school training, family seminars), Highwood Books (Books, printing, electronic and multimedia and a health-food store) and Highwood Communications (newsletter, stewardship, publicity).

Key to any vision is the organization's integrity to God's Word. It is because every other institution in the past history of the world has slowly in some cases, and suddenly in others, changed its direction that the greatest divinely-guided vigilance must be sought in order to ensure the integrity of the institution. Satan has been able to redirect the beliefs and principles of the founders or their successors. Satan has been able, step by nefarious step, to destroy the principles and God-given standards which are bastions against the inroads of evil. In these last days this must not be permitted to happen. If each worker remains true to God, it will not happen, for God will sweep Satan and his nefarious angels off the property.

We believe that once a year there should be a review by the members of every organization to address honestly the vision of the institution. If even in a small way that vision has changed, it is probable that it is moving toward apostasy. It is wavering from its original vision. Of course it may be argued unconvincingly that we are improving the vision or simply expanding it. However a true vision cannot be expanded. Yes, the activities to forward that vision can be expanded, but a divinely inspired vision can never be modified without beginning a process of change to the very fabric of that vision and thereby derailing it.

It is our hope that the present generation of lay- and self-supporting ministers will first carefully decide the vision based solely upon the Word of divine Inspiration. Make sure that the vision has not changed either in statement or in practice. Above all, this can be accomplished only if every addition to the membership of the staff is fully in harmony with that vision. So much is at stake today that we cannot afford to permit this generation of ministries to fail. We must have a sanctified commitment to do what no other generation of ministries has done in the history of the earth. We must unwaveringly remain wholly faithful to the vision which God has placed upon us until the close of human probation. That is our challenge; it is the challenge for each of the readers of this handbook.

God bless you.

SUMMARY

1   All God-raised up institutions during the history of the world have failed God.
2   During the closing years of this world's history schools of an entirely different order are to be instituted, different from those schools the Seventh-day Adventist Church has established in our past history.
3   These schools of a different order can succeed only when,
    a. Following a perfect Biblical pattern,
    b. Founded upon an enduring vision of God's perfect plan,
    c. All workers at the institution share the vision, therefore all must be chosen with the utmost care, and
    d. The core vision and ideology remains unshaken ir-

respective of sociological or theological changes in the world and church.
4. All institutions must increase in the scope of their ministry or they will eventually die.
5. At least once a year the whole staff should evaluate honestly,
   a. Has the integrity of the vision and ideology remained untarnished?
   b. What can be accomplished to more accurately reflect God's vision for the institution?
   c. What can be planned to increase the soul-winning endeavors?
   d. Above all, each individual staff member must daily evaluate his or her total surrender to Christ seeking to be ready to receive the empowering of the latter rain.

HARTLAND PUBLICATIONS
PUBLISHED BOOK LIST

HARTLAND PUBLICATIONS PUBLISHED BOOK LIST

Books by Colin and Russell Standish
(Unless otherwise noted as by one or the other)

Adventism Imperiled—Education In Crisis $11.95 PB 230 pgs.
In this newly revised edition of the most penetrating books written on Adventist education, the Standish Brothers go directly to the word of God for the principles by which children that are called to be the sons and daughters of the King of the Universe are to be educated. Every Seventh-day Adventist interested in our children and youth should read this book. Both authors are trained educators, having spent decades in education from the elementary to university level.

Adventism Proclaimed $9.95 PB 202 pgs.
In Answer to "When shall these things be and what shall be the sign of thy coming, and the end of the world?" (Matthew 24:3), Jesus related many signs. One of those signs (verse 14) has captivated the authors – "This gospel of the kingdom shall be preached in all the world for a witness unto all nations: and then shall the end come." In the context of the 3 Angels Messages, this is what shall go forth with the power of the Loud Cry of Revelation 18:1-5. "To every nation, and kindred, and tongue and people" (Revelation 14:6). You will feel compelled to share with others, and be motivated to prepare urgently for the coming of the Lord.

Adventism Vindicated $9.95 PB 141 pgs.
The late 1970s was a time when the new theology was rapidly engulfing a confused and uncertain Seventh-day Adventist Church as a reaction to legalistic principles. Tragically, many who found the impotency of legalism were deceived into accepting a theology that claims that there are no divine conditions of salvation–a belief that victorious Christian living is not possible and has no mandate in salvation. This book answers the writings of Sequera as they relate to the precious message of "Christ our Righteousness" given at the 1888 General Conference in Minneapolis.

The Antichrist Is Here $10.95 PB 185 pgs.
A newly updated, second edition! Colin and Russell Standish have extensively researched the historical identification of the Antichrist of past generations and are convinced the Antichrist is present on earth now. A "must read" for those who are interested in Biblical prophecy and its out-working in contemporary history.

The Big Bang Exploded $11.95 PB 218 pgs.
A refutation of the Big Bang theory and Darwin's proposal of natural selection, which boldly presents evidence that the authors assert supports, far more closely, the fiat creation concept than the evolutionary model

Deceptions of the New Theology $10.95 PB 290 pgs.
The term "new theology" was made prominent in the 1970s with the presentation by a number of popular preachers in the Seventh-day Adventist Church who taught what appeared to many to be a beautiful, new, Christ-centered emphasis. However, the ultimate results have been seen in untold thousands leaving the Seventh-day Adventist church, including many ministers and denominational workers. The answer to the eternal destructiveness of this movement is to uphold the authentic Christ.

Education for Excellence $11.95 PB 176 pgs.
This book goes directly to the word of God for educational principles for the sons and daughters of the King of the Universe.

Embattled Church $8.95 PB 143 pgs.
The SDA church faces a crisis! Confusion and division are rampant. Assurance of truth has surrendered to uncertainty. Surety of faith has given way to an enfeebling pluralism. Uniqueness has been overcome by ecumenicalism. The sense of urgency has been replaced by carnal security. The spiritual church has become a social club. Unwavering loyalty is now branded as bigotry. Faithfulness to Christ is judged legalism. The defenders of truth are spurned as schismatics. The state of the church has led untold thousands to reevaluate their relationship to it. This book addresses this issue of separation.

The Entertainment Syndrome $8.95 PB 126 pgs.
This book explores how the large increase in entertainment impacts the physical, emotional, social, intellectual and spiritual life of the human race, and the devastating effect of its use in our churches.

The Evangelical Dilemma $10.95 PB 222 pgs.
There has never been a more urgent time for an honest review of the past, present and future of Evangelical Protestantism. The authors present an examination of the major doctrinal errors of Evangelical Protestants.

The Gathering Storm and The Storm Burst $16.95 PB 421 pgs.
The Gathering Storm—The Seventh-day Adventist Church experienced a tragic and dramatic redirection of its doctrines and practices beginning in the mid-1950s. While many were aware of this, few knew the almost unbelievable story behind this great apostasy. In this section, formerly entitled *Adventism Challenged A*, the authors have traced the only authen-

tic, comprehensive development of this tragic area in God's remnant Church. Remarkably, God placed them in situations that allowed them to be eyewitnesses to the unfolding events. This book will challenge every reader who is loyal to Christ to rise up on behalf of God, His Word and His Truth.

The Storm Burst — The ease with which previous heresies successfully invaded the Seventh-day Adventist Church had been of great shock to all faithful members. Though we have been warned constantly that it would happen, its reality has come as a whirlwind into our midst. *Adventism Challenged B* continues to detail how the new theology was imported from Australia to the United States and other parts of the world. The authors document the earnest efforts of many current leaders, former leaders, and laity, to stay the plague of unfaithfulness to the truth and mission of the SDA Church.

Georgia Sits On Grandpa's Knee (R. Standish) $7.95 PB 86 pgs.
Stories for children based on the experience of Russell and his children in the mission field.

God's Solution for Depression, Guilt and Mental Illness $12.95 PB 229 pgs.
This powerful book argues with great persuasiveness that God is interested in every aspect of His created beings and that the perfect answers to man's needs are to be found in the Word of God.

Grandpa, You're Back! (R. Standish) $9.95 PB 128 pgs.
Pastor Russell Standish again delights and fascinates his granddaughter, Georgia, with stories of his many travels to countries ranging from South America to such far-flung places as Singapore, Africa, and beyond. These stories should pleasantly awake the imagination of young readers.

Gwanpa and Nanny's Home (R. Standish and Ella Rankin) $14.95 PB 128 pgs.
"I am Ella Marie Rankin. I want to tell you about Gwanpa's and Nanny's home. But I have a problem! You see, I'm only three and I haven't yet learned to write. So, my Gwanpa is writing my story for me." So begins a book that Russell Standish wrote for his granddaughter.

Holy Relics or Revelation $14.95 PB 300 pgs.
Biblical archaeologists have gathered data with painstaking effort, and their work proves the accuracy of the Bible. Yet, mostly within a single decade, Ron Wyatt had sought out and claimed the most amazing Biblical sites and relics. In this book, the Standish Brothers examine the Wyatt claims in-depth. Their findings serve as a benchmark upon which Ron Wyatt's "discoveries" can be more carefully evaluated.

Keepers of the Faith $12.95 PB 240 pgs.
As every wind of doctrine is marshaled against the church, more determined efforts are required to alert and warn of the dangers and errors that are now endemic in most congregations. In this book, the authors have attempted to identify and explain clearly the nature of many of these errors, and to document the clear truth as revealed by Inspiration. The book is especially directed to gospel ministers and lay leaders in the church. Previous editions of the book have found wide circulation among rank-and-file laity who discovered it to be one of the clearest presentations of Biblical principles of truth and righteousness.

Liberty in the Balance $14.95 PB 263 pgs.
The bloodstained pathway to religious and civil liberty faces its greatest test in 200 years. The United States "Bill of Rights" lifted the concept of liberty far beyond the realm of toleration to an inalienable right for all citizens. Yet, for a century and a half, some students of the prophecies of John the Revelator have foretold a time just prior to the return of Christ when these most cherished freedoms will be wrenched from the

citizens of the United States, and the U.S. would enforce its coercive edicts upon the rest of the world. This book traces the courageous battle for freedom, a battle stained with the lives of many martyrs.

The Lord's Day $15.95 PB 310 pgs.
The issue of the apostolic origin of Sunday worship had often been a contentious one between Roman Catholics and Protestants. This book presents an in-depth examination of the Sabbath in Scriptures.

Modern Bible Translations Unmasked $10.95 PB 228 pgs.
This book will challenge the reader to consider two very serious problems with modern Bible translations: first, the use of corrupted Greek manuscripts; and second, translational bias. This is a must read for anyone interested the veracity and accuracy of the Word of God. (Supplement for SDA members) - $3.95 PB 28 pgs.

The Mystery of Death $10.95 PB 128 pgs.
There are those today who believe that the soul is immortal and externally preexisted the body. Pagan or Christian, the opinions vary widely. In this book, the history of these concepts is reviewed and the words of Scripture are investigated for a definitive and unchallengeable answer.

Organizational Structure and Apostasy $11.95 PB 164 pgs.
This new reprint of *The Temple Cleansed* specifically details the way the organizational structure of the SDA Church is being molded after the deadly hierarchal pattern of the world. Few understand the simple organizational pattern that God provided for His church at all denominational and local levels—therefore, few raise the alarm. The eyes of the discerning reader should be opened to the type of organization God will have in place when he cleanses His church. The human machinery will be swept aside.

Perils of Ecumenism $15.95 PB 416 pgs.
The march of ecumenism seems unstoppable. From its humble roots after the first World War, with the formation of the Faith and Order Council at Edinburgh University, Scotland, and the Works and Labor Council at Oxford University, England, to the formation of the World Council of Churches in 1948 in Amsterdam, it has gained breathtaking momentum. The authors see the ecumenical movement as very clearly identified in Holy Scriptures as the movement devised by the arch-deceiver to beguile the inhabitants of the world.

Perils of Time Setting $7.95 PB 82 pgs.
This book demonstrates the failure of every time setting prediction ever made since 1844. It gives conclusive evidence that such time setting has its foundations in the Jesuit scheme to derail the Protestant Reformation and to refocus Protestants from their unwavering identification of the Papacy as the historical Antichrist of prophecy. It is an invaluable guide as to how to avoid being trapped by tantalizing but false principles of biblical interpretation.

The Pope's Letter and Sunday Law $7.95 PB 116 pgs.
This book presents a detailed examination of John Paul II's apostolic letter, "Dies Domini."

The Rapture and the Antichrist $14.95 PB 288 pgs.
This book sets forth the plainest truths of Scripture directing Protestantism back to its Biblical roots. It will challenge the thinking of all Christians, erase the fictions of the *Left Behind* Series, and plant the reader's spiritual feet firmly on the platform of Scripture.

The Rapture, the End Times and the Millennium $15.99 PB 378 pgs.
This book will open the minds of the readers to a clear understanding of areas of the end-time which have led to much perplexity among lay-people and theologians alike. It is also guaranteed to dispel many of the perplexities presently con-

fronting those who are searching for a clear Biblical exposition of the last cataclysmic days in which we now live.

The Road to Rome $9.95 PB 217 pgs
Sister White wrote, "The Omega of Apostasy will be of a most startling nature." (SM, Vol. 1, pg. 197). She also stated–"The church has turned back from following Christ, her Leader, and is steadily retreating toward Egypt." (1T, pg. 217). The time is overdue for us to evaluate how far we have traveled down the Road To Rome! With deep sensitivity and a passionate love for their church, the authors have uncovered what many will recognize as an orchestrated plan to systematically implement the catholicizing of the Seventh-day Adventist Church.

The Sacrificial Priest $15.95 PB 272 pgs.
To all Christians the centrality of the sacrifice of Christ on Calvary has been the focus of their salvation hopes. However, relatively few Christians have understood the equally important ministry of Christ in the heavenly sanctuary. The authors provide a fascinating Biblical explanation and irrefutable evidence of this little-studied high priestly ministry of Christ in the heavenly sanctuary.

The Second Coming $7.95 PB 80 pgs.
The Apostle Paul refers to the second coming of Jesus as the blessed hope (Titus 2:12). Yet, soon after the death of all the apostles, doubts and debates robbed the people of this assurance and brought in the pagan notion of immediate life after death. In this new updated work, Colin and Russell Standish present a "wake-up call" for every complacent Christian.

The Sepulchres Are Whited $7.95 PB 301 pgs.
We are at the end of probationary time. If God's church is to receive the full outpouring of the latter rain, there must be a return to truth and righteousness. This alone will provide the unity that God can honor with His Spirit. This book is written to stimulate such a reformation in our ranks.

Spiritism in the SDA Church $7.95 PB 133 pgs.
The authors believe that every deviation from truth has its root in spiritism. They take a broad concept of spiritism to include idolatry, paganism, humanism, New Age philosophy, Catholicism and Satanism, and explore some surprisingly "respectable" forms of spiritism that are designed especially for the more wary Christian. This book reveals the frightening inroads of spiritualistic theory and practice that has become deeply embedded within much of contemporary Seventh-day Adventism.

Swarming Independents $8.95 PB 118 pgs.
Self-supporting ministries, independent ministries, supporting ministries–sometimes there seems to be utter confusion in the Seventh-day Adventist church today about their roles. Some church members believe that the denominational work is so paralyzed by apostasy, worldliness, and corruption that lay ministries are the only hope for finishing the gospel commission. Others militantly oppose lay ministries, labeling them as schismatics, dividers, "separatists," cultists, and offshoots. What is the truth?

Tithes and Offerings — Trampling The Conscience $9.95 PB 112 pgs.
With unreasonable fervor and scant knowledge, many have sought to condemn God's ordained self-supporting ministries that accept tithe for their soul saving gospel work. This has led the tithe issue to become a religious liberty issue in God's Church. This book is a remarkable contribution to our understanding of this topic. The authors have researched the tithe issue to a depth never before attempted, and have again done what they do best–bring an issue back to the objective evidence of God's sacred Word and the Spirit of Prophecy.

Two Beasts, Three Deadly Wounds and Fourteen Popes $16.95 PB 234 pgs.
The Book of Revelation has been characterized as a mystery. Yet, the book describes itself as the "Revelation of Jesus Christ"

(Revelation 1:1). In this book, the authors, using Scripture as its own interpreter, unravel aspects of the "mystery" and unveil a portion of the revelation.

Winds of Doctrine $12.95 PB 168 pgs.
Satan has not confined his attacks to denominational workers and leaders, but has also attacked those in the self-supporting work. The tragedy is that some have accepted the nefarious subtleties of Satan and have led many that are not stabilized in the faith away from truth and righteousness. This book is essential reading for all earnest Seventh-day Adventists. It takes up the issues central to the apostasy – the name of God, the Godhead, the Person of the Holy Spirit, the eternal existence of Christ, the Wednesday crucifixion, the correct Sabbath hours, and God's destructive judgment.

The Vision and God's Providence (C. Standish) $14.95 PB 240 pgs.
The story of the development of Hartland Institute must be attributed to God alone. Yet, many men and women have had the privilege of being His humble instruments in contributing to Hartland's establishment. This book recalls divine leadings, human weaknesses, misunderstandings, and strong differences of opinion, and we cannot but wonder what God might have accomplished, had we listened perfectly to His voice.

Youth Do You Dare! (C. Standish) $6.95 PB 74 pgs.
If you are a young person looking for workable answers to the many issues that confront you today, this book is for you. It presents a call to young people to follow truth and righteousness, and to live morally upright lives.

Other Books from Hartland Publications

Behold the Lamb - David Kang $8.95 PB 107 pgs.
God's plan of redemption for this world and the preservation of the universe is revealed in the sanctuary which God constructed through Moses. This book explains the sanctuary service in light of the Christian's personal experience. Why this book? Because Jesus is coming soon!

China Letters - David Lin $14.95 PB 428 pgs.
Applies the hammer of truth to the tensile of New Theology, exposing the nature of the base metal for what really is, not gold or silver, but rather tin and dross. These collected letters and articles appeared in various Adventist periodicals at a time when Ford's teachings were the center of attention in the SDA church.

Christ and Antichrist - Samuel J. Cassels $24.95 HB 348 pgs.
First published in 1846 by a well-known Presbyterian minister, who called this book "not sectarian, but a Christian and Protestant work." He hoped that the removal of obstacles might result in a more rapid spread of the Gospel. One of these obstacles he saw as "Antichristianity," a term he that he used to describe the Papal system.

Distinctive Vegetarian Cuisine - Sue M. Weir $14.95 PB 329 pgs.
100% vegan cooking, with no animal products—no meat, milk, eggs, cheese, or even honey. No irritating spices or condiments are used. Most of the ingredients can be found at your local market. There are additional nutritional information and helpful hints. Make your dinner table appealing to the appetite!

Food for Thought - Susan Jen $10.95 PB 160 pgs.
Where does the energy which food creates come from? What kinds of foods are the most conducive to robust health and well being in all dimensions of our life? What is a balanced

diet? Written by a healthcare professional, this book examines the food we prepare for our table.

Group Think - Horace E. Walsh $5.95 PB 96 pgs.
Find out how a state of groupthink (or group dynamics) has often contributed to disaster in secular and spiritual matters, like the role of Hebrew groupthink in the rejection and ultimate crucifixion of the Son of God. Or, the Ecumenical Movement that seeks to unite the minds of dedicated men so much that their passion is to build one great super church following Rome.

Heroes of the Reformation - Hagstotz and Hagstotz $14.95 PB 320 pgs.
This volume brings together a comprehensive picture of the leaders of the Reformation who arose all over Europe. The authors of this volume have made a sincere endeavor to bring the men of Protestantism alive in the hearts of this generation.

His Mighty Love - Ralph Larson $9.95 PB 159 pgs.
Twenty-one evangelistic sermons! Every doctrine of the Bible is simply an answer to the question, "How does the love of God relate to this particular question or problem?" Every doctrine is further evidence that God is love! This book is divided into three sections with seven individual sermons each. Subjects range from "If God Is Almighty, Why Does He Permit Sin?" to "The Unpardonable Sin."

History of the Gunpowder Plot - Philip Sidney $13.95 PB 303 pgs.
Originally published on the 300th anniversary of the November 5, 1605, plot aimed at the destruction of the English Realm, is Philip Sydney's account of one of the most audacious conspiracies ever known to the ancient or modern world. The failed plot became part of English popular culture.

The History of Protestantism - J. A. Wylie $99.95 PB 4 Volumes
This book pulls back the divine curtain and reveals God's hand in the affairs of His church during the Protestant Reformation. Your heart will be stirred by the lives of Protestant heroes, and your mind captivated by God's simple means to counteract the intrigues of its enemies. As God's church faces the last days, this compelling book will appeal to, and be a blessing to adults as well as children.

History of the Reformation of the 16th Century - J. d'Aubigné $19.95   PB 876 pgs.
In history and in prophecy, the Word of God portrays the long continued conflict between truth and error. Today, we see an alarming lack of understanding in the Protestant Church concerning the cause and effect of the Reformation. This reprinted masterpiece pulls back the curtain of history and divine providence to reveal the true catalyst for the Reformation—God's Word and His Holy Spirit.

History of the Reformation in the Time of Calvin - J. d'Aubigné $129.95 4 Vol.
The renovation of the individual, of the Church, and of the human race, is the theme. This renovation is, at the same time, an enfranchisement; and we might assign, as a motto to the Reformation accomplished by Calvin, as well as to apostolical Christianity itself, these words of Jesus Christ: The truth shall make you free (John 8:32).

History of the Waldenses - J. A. Wylie $12.95 PB 191 pgs.
During the long centuries of papal supremacy, the Waldenses defied the crushing power of Rome and rejected its false doctrines and traditions. This stalwart people cherished and preserved the pure Word of God. It is fitting that this edition of their history should be reprinted to keep alive the spirit and knowledge of this ancient people.

Hus the Heretic - Poggius the Papist $9.95 PB 78 pgs.
One of the greatest of Reformers in history was John Hus. His pious life and witness during his trial and martyrdom convinced many of the priests and church leaders of his innocence and the justice of his cause. Poggius was the papal legate who delivered the summons to Hus to appear at the council of Constance, then participated as a member. This book consists of letters from Poggius to his friend Nikolai, and describes the trial and burning of Hus. So potent was John Hus' humble testimony, that even some of his ardent foes became his defenders.

The Law and the Sabbath - Allen Walker $9.95 PB 149 pgs.
A fierce controversy is swirling around the role the Ten Commandments should play in the church of the 21st Century. With a foreword by the late Elder Joe Crews, here is a book that dares to examine the Bible's own answers—with unfailing scriptural logic and a profound appreciation for the doctrine of righteousness by faith.

The Method of Grace - John Flavel $14.95 PB 458 pgs.
In this faithful reprint, John Flavel thoroughly outlines the work of God's Spirit in applying the redemptive work of Christ to the believer. Readers will find their faith challenged and enriched. In true Puritan tradition, a clearly defined theology is delivered with evangelistic fervor, by an author urgently concerned about the eternal destiny of the human soul.

My Escape from the Auto de Fé - Don Fernando de la Mina $9.95 PB 112 pgs.
In the difficult days of the Reformation in Spain, Nobleman Don Fernando de la Mina was arrested by the Inquisitors and sentenced to death for "heresy." He was about to be burned at the stake at the Auto de Fé (act of faith), when, through several incredible miracles of Providence, he made his escape. This captivating story will strengthen your faith in the protecting hand over God's faithful believers.

The Reformation in Spain - Thomas M'Crie $13.95 PB 272 pgs.
The boldness with which Luther attacked the abuses and the authority of the Church in Rome in the 16th Century attracted attention throughout Christendom. Luther's writings, along with the earlier ones of Erasmus, gained a foothold with a Spanish people hungry for the truth. Thomas M'Crie makes a case for a Spain free of the religious errors and corruptions that ultimately dried up the resources and poisoned the fountains of a great empire.

Romanism and the Reformation - H. Grattan Guinness $12.95 PB 217 pgs.
The Reformation of the 16th Century, which gave birth to Protestantism, was based on Scripture. It gave back to the world the Bible. Such Reformation work needs to be done again today. The duty of diffusing information on the true character and history of "Romanism and the Reformation" is one that presses on God's faithful people in these days.

Strange Fire - Barry Harker $11.95 PB 206 pgs.
The Olympic games are almost universally accepted as a great international festival of peace, sportsmanship, and friendly competition. Yet, the games are riddled with conflict, cheating, and objectionable competitiveness. Discover the disturbing truth about the modern Olympics and the role of Christianity in the rise of this neo-pagan religion.

The Third Angel's Message of Righteousness by Faith and Its Present Rejection - L. Scarborough $6.95 PB 107 pgs.
As SDAs, we tend to believe that our greatest danger of being deceived by error would come from without the church. Our concerns have been concentrated upon these varied forms of deceptions. We are far less prepared to stand against the deceptions that will come from within our own church.

Truth Triumphant - Benjamin George Wilkinson $14.95 PB 419 pgs.
The prominence given to the "Church in the Wilderness" in the Scriptures establishes without argument its existence and emphasizes its importance. The same challenges exist today with the Remnant Church in its final controversy against the powers of evil to show the holy, unchanging message of the Bible.

With Cloak and Dagger - H. H. Meyers $9.95 PB 213 pgs.
This is a startling revelation of a deliberate and successful effort by a small group of men to effectively sabotage the message and mission of God's remnant church. The basic fundamental principles that were endorsed by God's prophet to His remnant church as having "unquestionable authority," have since been systematically eroded and even changed!

Who Are These Three Angels? - Jeff Wehr $6.95 PB 126 pgs.
The messages of three holy angels unfold for us events that are soon to take place. Their warning is not to be taken lightly. They tell of political and religious movements that signal the soon return of Jesus.

The Word Was Made Flesh - Ralph Larson $11.95 PB 365 pgs.
One hundred years of Seventh-day Adventist Christology, from 1852 to 1952. This book is a comprehensive survey of the historical evidence of the human nature of Christ. "The nature of God, whose law had been transgressed, and the nature of Adam, the transgressor, meet in Jesus, the Son of God, and the Son of Man." Ellen White, *Manuscript 141*, 1901.

Youth Ministry in Crisis - Barry Harker $10.95 206 pgs.
In this bracing book, Dr. Barry Harker examines the practices and passions that are transforming and debasing contemporary youth ministry—rock music, magic, clowning, comedy, drama, mime, puppetry, sports, extreme adventure activities, youth fashions and movies – and exposes the disturbing ideas

that permit them to flourish in God's church. Dr. Harker also outlines steps that need to be taken if the enveloping crisis is to be resolved and youth ministry restored to a culture of defensible innovation. This book is a timely corrective to the ideas and practices that are defacing the image of God in His people.

True Education History Series from Hartland Publications

The Waldenses—The Church in the Wilderness $7.95 PB 72 pgs.
The faithful Waldenses in their mountain retreats were married in a spiritual sense to God who promised, "I will betroth thee unto me in faithfulness and thou shalt know the Lord" (Hosea 2:20). No invention of Satan could destroy their union with God. Follow the history of these people as they are compared to the dedicated eagle parents.

David Livingstone—The Pathfinder - Basil Matthews $8.95 PB 112 pgs.
Like most boys and girls, David Livingstone wondered what he would become when he grew up. He had heard of a brave man who was a missionary doctor in China. He also learned that this Dr. Gulztoff had a Hero, Jesus, who had come to people as a healer and missionary. David learned all about this great Physician, and felt that the finest thing in the whole world for him was to follow in the same way and be a medical missionary. That was David's quest, which was his plan. Between these pages, you shall see how he made his good wish come true.

Missionary Annuls—Memoir of Robert Moffat - M. L. Wilder $7.95 PB 64 pgs.
Robert Moffat first heard from his wise and pious mother's lips that there were heathen in the world and of the efforts of Christians sharing the knowledge of a Savior who could raise them out of their base degradation. An intense desire took possession of him to serve God in some marked manner but how that would be, he did not know. Through a series of providential circumstances and in God's good time, the London Society accepted him as one of their missionaries, and in 1816, he embarked on his first trip and got his first glimpse of heathen Africa. This book will inspire young and

old as you read the many trials, disappointments, triumphs, and wondrous miracles that God can accomplish when one is fully surrendered to Him.

About the Authors

COLIN AND RUSSELL STANDISH were born in Newcastle, Australia, in 1933. They both obtained their teaching diplomas from Avondale College in 1951. They were appointed to one-teacher Seventh-day Adventist primary (elementary) schools in rural areas of New South Wales, each teaching for three years.

Both in 1958 completed a major in history and undertook an honors degree in psychology at Sydney University in the field of learning theory. Colin continued in this area, obtaining his Master of Arts degree with honors in 1961, and his Doctor of Philosophy in 1964. In 1967 he completed a Masters Degree in Education.

Russell graduated as a physician in 1964. Six years later he was admitted to the Royal College of Physicians (UK) by examination. He was elevated to the Fellowship of the Royal Colleges of Physicians in Edinburgh (1983) and Glasgow (1984).

In 1965, Colin was appointed Chairman of the Education Department at Avondale College. Subsequently he held the posts of Academic Dean at West Indies College (1970), President of West Indies College (1970-73), Chairman of the Department of Psychology, Columbia Union College (1974), President of Columbia Union College (1974-78), Dean of Weimar College (1978-83). He was invited to become the foundational president of Hartland Institute, which consists of a degree-issuing college, a wellness center, publishing house and a world mission division.

Russell as a Consultant Physician (Internist) has held the posts of Deputy Medical Superintendent of the Austin Hospital, University of Melbourne (1975-1978), President of the Bangkok Adventist Hospital (!979-1984), Medical Director at Enton Medical Centre, England (1984-1986), President of Penang Adventist Hospital (1986-1989), and Director of Health Services in the Southeast Asia Union (1989-1992). Since 1992 he has been speaker and editor for Remnant Herald.

Both Colin (1970) and Russell (1980) were ordained to the Seventh-day Adventist ministry. Both have been appointed delegates to General Conference Sessions—Colin in 1975 and Russell in 1980 and 1990. They have co-authored forty books.

HARTLAND PUBLICATIONS was established in 1984 as a conservative, self supporting Protestant publishing house. We publish Bible-based books and produce media for Christians of all ages, to help them in the development of their personal characters, always giving glory to God in preparation for the soon return of our Lord and Savior, Christ Jesus. We are especially dedicated to the reprinting of significant books on Protestant history that might otherwise go out of circulation. Hartland Publications supports and promotes other Christian publishers and media producers who are consistent with biblical principles of truth and righteousness. We are seeking to arouse the spirit of true Protestantism, one that is based on the Bible and the Bible only, thus awakening the world to a sense of the value and privilege of the religious liberty that we currently enjoy.

Hartland Publications

Office hours: 9:00 am, to 5:00 p.m. Mon.— Thurs., 9:00 a.m. to 12:00 noon Fri. (Eastern time)

You may order by telephone, fax, mail, e-mail or on the website.
Payments in $US by check, money order, most credit cards.

Order line: 1-800-774-3566 FAX 1-540-672-3568

Website: www.hartlandpublications.com
E-mail:sales@hartlandpublications.org